AN INTRODUCTION TO EXPERIMENTAL DESIGN
IN PSYCHOLOGY: A CASE APPROACH

AN INTRODUCTION TO

HARPER'S EXPERIMENTAL PSYCHOLOGY SERIES
UNDER THE EDITORSHIP OF H. PHILIP ZEIGLER

EXPERIMENTAL DESIGN IN PSYCHOLOGY: A CASE APPROACH

HOMER H. JOHNSON AND ROBERT L. SOLSO

Loyola University of Chicago

HARPER & ROW, PUBLISHERS

NEW YORK, EVANSTON, SAN FRANCISCO, LONDON

An Introduction to Experimental Design in Psychology: A Case Approach

Copyright © 1971 by Homer H. Johnson and Robert L. Solso

Standard Book Number: 06-043332-9

Library of Congress Catalog Card Number: 71-168358

CONTENTS

TO THE INSTRUCTOR

This book was designed as a supplementary text for use in introductory psychology or introductory experimental psychology courses, although it also may be applicable for higher-level courses. Our purpose in writing the book was our feeling that the basic principles of experimental design can be taught rather easily by using fairly simple examples of research. Too often the teaching of design is obscured by lengthy discussions of philosophy of science or by concentrating on one or two highly specialized areas of psychology. To avoid these problems we have eliminated any discussion of the former, and have provided examples from various areas of psychology. It is our feeling that through the use of this text the student will learn basic design principles fairly quickly as well as learn quite a bit about some content areas of psychology.

It would be inappropriate for us to tell the instructor how the text should be used; however, we would like to note briefly how we have used these materials with students having only a minimal knowledge of psychology. Our procedure was to make daily reading assignments of a small amount of material and to discuss this material during the next class session. Chapter 1 is introductory material and was usually handled in one class session. Chapter 2 was usually discussed in four or five class sessions. The first three sections of this chapter were usually understood by the students without much help from the instructor, but some students needed help with the later sections. In Chapter 3 the four control-problem examples were discussed at length in class to insure that the student understood the design and procedures involved.

The design critiques in Chapter 4 were handled in two ways. One way was to have the students redesign the experiments outside of class and select students to present their designs in class. The rest of the class was asked to comment on, and to criticize, the new design. A second method used is similar to the first except the students were put in groups of threes or fours and the group presented the new designs. This latter procedure generates considerably more discussion and debate since groups seem to become more involved in their product than do individuals.

In the class discussion of Chapter 5, initial emphasis was placed on the problems (through examples) that could arise if a biased assignment of subjects occurs. This emphasizes why the various assignment procedures are used and the emphasis on the problem seems to generate more appreciation of possible solutions. The procedure for Chapter 6 was similar to that of Chapter 4; however, we usually spent less time on the discussion of new designs.

The last eight chapters of the book are reprinted experiments plus comments. The experiments become increasingly difficult and it is advisable to take them in the order of presentation in the book. For beginning students of psychology it is important that some of the experiments be discussed thoroughly even to the point of reading them aloud in class and discussing the article point by point. Reading the psychological literature is a new and somewhat anxiety-provoking experience for most students. A thorough discussion of the articles seems to relieve much of this anxiety as well as acquaint the student with design and technique in a specific content area.

Our goal in this book is to make psychological research more understandable, more interesting, and perhaps exciting to the student. We encourage communication from instructors as to how we might better achieve these goals within the context of a book such as this. Finally, we would express our appreciation to our patient and skillful secretary, Mrs. Nell Finch. We are especially grateful to H. Philip Zeigler who provided valuable advice and guidance throughout this venture.

I

BASIC PRINCIPLES IN EXPERIMENTAL DESIGN

1

AN INTRODUCTION TO SCIENTIFIC INQUIRY

WHAT IS SCIENCE?

If the layman is asked "What is science?" the usual answer is that science is physics, chemistry, and biology. Thus, it would appear that science is defined by certain specific subject areas. There is some support for this definition of science. For example, college students have to take a number of required "science courses," and these courses usually are drawn from physics, chemistry, and biology. However, this definition does not appear to be adequate. If you ask why chemistry is a science but history is not, or why physics is a science but English is not, the definition of science becomes more complex and usually quite confusing. People usually say something about science dealing with facts (yet, so does history), or science dealing with theories (so does history), or that science involves laboratory experiments (but what about astronomy or the classification of plants in biology). This is usually where the discussion ends, with the layman saying that he does not know exactly how to answer the question.

The layman's difficulty with an adequate definition of science is also shared by the scientist. There are various definitions of science. Many of these specify the collection of facts, the use of experimentation as a method of "proof," the use of theories as tentative explanations, etc. Some definitions emphasize the on-going or dynamic nature of science—the search for and discovery of new "facts," and new theories arising to replace the old much as the theories of Einstein replaced those of Newton. James Conant (1951, p. 25) expresses this quality of science when he defines science as "an interconnected series of concepts and conceptual schemes that have developed as a result of experimentation and observation and are fruitful of further experimentation and observation." By observation and experimentation, the scientist attempts to ascertain what is related to what, or what "cause" is related to what "effect." These "facts" are put into conceptual schemes. These schemes (or theories, or models) are tentative; they are the best way we can explain or interrelate the information we have on hand. New information, and then new conceptual schemes, will arise to replace the old. There is always more information to explain and new "facts" to be discovered. This is the dynamic quality of science.

WHY A SCIENCE OF PSYCHOLOGY?

Perhaps the reader is wondering, as Underwood (1957) so aptly put it, "Why this fixation or fetish on the application of scientific method to psychological problems?" The answer is quite simple. Psychologists attempt to understand the lawfulness of behavior; and to understand, to predict, or to control behavior with any precision is a very difficult task. Scientific inquiry seems to offer the possibility of handling such a task, and psychologists adopt it simply because it is the best approach we have which may give us the precision we want.

The layman also understands behavior; at least, he understands behavior to the extent that he can coexist with other people. He has principles of behavior; for example, "absence makes the heart grow fonder." But there is a contrary principle that goes "out of sight, out of mind." To *predict* precisely which of these principles will hold in a given case is beyond the layman's ability. Furthermore, his understanding of behavior is highly colored by his own perspectives. Campus disturbances, for example, are called everything from left-wing plots, to right-wing plots, to anarchist plots, depending on one's perspectives (and anxieties). The layman's beliefs about black Americans in many parts of the country involve a variety of assumptions about "innate" motivations, "innate" sexual drives, "innate" abilities (e.g., musical), etc. This basic understanding of a group of people is highly distorted by one's prejudices and cultural background. The layman does not engage in a systematic study of behavior; he does not formulate hypotheses about behavior and then test these hypotheses; he does not test his conceptual schemes in any organized manner. But the psychologist does and the techniques the psychologist uses are designed to test his hypotheses, and these techniques can be loosely described as scientific inquiry.

ON "THE SCIENTIFIC METHOD"

It is obvious from the earlier discussion that an exact definition of science cannot be given. Rather, the activity of science was described in somewhat vague terms. The same problem arises when one attempts to define "the scientific method." Some authors seem to imply that *the* scientific method consists of a few simple steps which, if followed, will lead to amazing and dramatic discoveries about nature. If there is *a* method of science, why does science progress in such a slow, fumbling, bumbling manner? A well-publicized example is the fact that we have attempted to find a cure for cancer for at least a half a century and, in spite of the use of some highly talented researchers and millions of dollars, the progress has been very slow.

The reality of the situation is that there is no such thing as *the* scientific method. It makes more sense to talk about methods of science or perhaps to talk about scientific methodology. Neither of these terms implies a single method or a single approach. Scientific inquiry consists of a variety of techniques, approaches, strategies, designs, and rules of logic. These vary from problem to problem and discipline to discipline. This book will attempt to give the reader an indication of some of these techniques as they have been used in psychology. Emphasis will be placed on experimental research in which the researcher manipulates some factors (variables), controls others, and ascertains the effects of the manipulated variable on another variable. This type of research best illustrates the researcher's attempts to control relevant variables and to find the cause and effect (functional) relationships between them. It is the search for such relationships which is so characteristic of scientific research.

In this chapter, an attempt was made to answer three questions frequently raised by students—"What is science?" "What is the scientific method?" "Why are psychologists so insistent on being scientific?" Although the answers have been brief, it is hoped that they will provide some general understanding and justification for what follows in this book. The next chapter will offer a more specific attempt to examine some of the basic concepts of experimental design.

2

DESIGN STRATEGIES

THE LOGIC OF EXPERIMENTAL DESIGN

An Italian scientist, named Spallanzani, attempted to determine what part of the semen stimulates the egg cell to develop into a fetus and then into a child. On the basis of some earlier results, Spallanzani hypothesized that it was the sperm cell. To test this hypothesis, Spallanzani artificially inseminated dogs with either the normal semen or the seminal fluid with the sperm cells filtered out. The bitches inseminated with the normal fluid became pregnant, whereas the bitches inseminated with the sperm-free filtrate did not become pregnant. Thus, Spallanzani demonstrated that it was the sperm cell which stimulated the egg cell to develop.

This experiment was conducted around 1785, and it was conducted by a biologist not a psychologist. However, in spite of its age and despite the fact that it was a biological experiment, Spallanzani's work illustrates basic principles of experimental design that are frequently used in psychology today. Spallanzani started with an hypothesis that was based on previous research. In order to test this hypothesis, he used an artificial insemination technique (actually, he invented the technique). By using this technique, he could *control* the insemination process and *manipulate* the content of the fluid prior to its injection into the dogs. Having this control, he set up a two-group experiment. One group of bitches (the experimental group) was inseminated with the sperm-free filtrate and another group of bitches (the control group) was inseminated with the normal semen. The two groups were treated alike in all other ways. Since the *only* difference between the two groups was in whether or not sperm cells were present in the seminal fluid, then any difference in the pregnancy rates between the two groups must have been due to this manipulation. It was this type of logic and this type of design that enabled Spallanzani to arrive at his (valid) conclusion.

Most psychological research uses the very same type of logic.

In the simplest case, one factor (*variable*) is manipulated by the experimenter and all other factors are held constant. The manipulated variable is called the *independent* variable, and the effects of this manipulation upon another variable called the *dependent* variable is observed. (In Spallanzani's experiment the dependent variable was the number of dogs that became pregnant.) Usually, one group of subjects receives one *level* (type or amount) of the independent variable, and another group of subjects receives another level of the independent variable. Since both groups of subjects are treated exactly alike *except* for the independent variable, then any difference observed in the dependent variable is due in all probability to the independent variable. In this manner, the psychologist hopes to precisely ascertain the effects of one variable on another and to build knowledge about cause and effect relationships (*functional relationships*) in behavior. Some writers have talked about this whole process in terms of a "theory of control." This label is a good expression of the idea behind research. An attempt is made to control variables either by manipulation or by holding them constant. Once this control is obtained, the determinants of behavior can be discovered.

With this overview of experimental logic, the following material will illustrate some of the basic concepts and designs used in psychological research.

INDEPENDENT AND DEPENDENT VARIABLES

It has already been noted that in the experimental situation we manipulate one variable and observe the effect of this manipulation on another variable. The manipulated variable is called the *independent* variable. The variable being observed is called the *dependent* variable. The experimenter simply measures the subjects' responses which thus constitute the dependent variable.

EXAMPLE

Lorge (1930) investigated the problem of whether performance on a task is better when a person practices the task continuously without interruption (massed practice), or when a person distributes his practice sessions with rest intervals in between them (spaced practice). Lorge chose for his task a mirror-tracing problem in which the subject traces a pattern (e.g., a star) but can only see the pattern (and his hand) in a mirror. Lorge had three groups of subjects, each group tracing the pattern 20 times. For one group of subjects the 20 trials were completed one after another with no rest between trials. For a second group of subjects each trial was followed by a 1-minute rest period. A third group of subjects practiced one trial a day for 20 days, thus there was a 24-hour interval between trials. His measure of performance was the length of time it took the subjects to trace the pattern—the shorter the time, the better was the performance. His results indicated that except for the first trial the average performance of the 24-hour interval group was better than that of the 1-minute interval group, and the 1-minute interval group was better than the continuous-practice group. The conclusion was that on this type of task, spaced practice leads to better performance than massed practice.

In the Lorge experiment the independent variable was a quantitative one, the length of time interval between trials—either zero minutes, 1 minute, or 24 hours. Note that the experimenter actively manipulated this variable. The dependent variable was the time it took the subjects to trace the pattern and the experimenter merely measured (or recorded) this variable. Lorge attempted to keep all other factors constant. For example, the subjects all performed the same task. They all had the same number of trials on the task. The task is rather unique and requires special equipment. Had the task involved learning lists of words the subjects might have gotten additional (uncontrolled) practice during rest periods.

EXAMPLE

Asch (1952) conducted an experiment to determine if the first information you receive about another person is more important in forming an impression of him than later information (*primacy effect*), or if later information is more important (*recency effect*). Asch used two groups of subjects. A series of adjectives which were said to describe a certain person were read to both groups; however, one group received positive information first and negative information last, while the second group received negative information first and the positive information last. The adjectives (and order) read to the group receiving positive information first were *intelligent, industrious, impulsive, critical, stubborn,* and *envious.* The group receiving the negative information first were read the same list but in reverse order. Asch then asked the subjects to write down their general impression of the person. The group receiving the positive information first described him as an able person who had certain short-comings. The group receiving the negative information first described him as a "problem" whose abilities were hampered by serious difficulties. Since the group that received the positive information first tended to have a positive evaluation of the stimulus person, and the group that received the negative information first tended to have a negative evaluation, Asch concluded that there is a primacy effect in impression formation.

The independent variable in the above example was the order of presentation of the information—either positive to negative, or negative to positive. The dependent variable was the subjects' descriptions of the person. All other variables were held constant, e.g., both groups received exactly the same adjectives. Since the only difference between the treatment groups was the order of presentation, then the different impressions must be due to this manipulation. Thus, Asch was able to demonstrate a "law of primacy" in the formation of impressions.

Frequently, experimenters will use a "*subject variable*" as an independent variable. A subject variable is a variable such as IQ, authoritarianism, sex, or some other trait or characteristic that a person "carries with him." For example, an experimenter may want to ascertain the effects of the personality trait of authoritarianism on concept learning, so he *selects* two groups of subjects. One group consists of people who receive high scores on a standard test for authoritarianism and one group who receive low scores on the same test. Both groups perform the same concept learning task, and the amount or speed of learning is the dependent variable. Note here that the experimenter has not actively *manipulated* authoritarianism but he has *selected* for it.

There are numerous subject variables that have been "selected" as independent variables. For example, children of wealthy parents and children of poor parents have been asked to draw pictures of dimes or quarters in order to examine the effects of economic background on estimates of size of money. There are many experiments that compare the responses of males versus females on a variety of tasks. A comparison of the incidence of lung cancer for people who smoke cigarettes versus people who do not smoke has been made. Frequency of lung cancer is the dependent variable and smoking is the independent variable that has been selected, not manipulated.

EXPERIMENTAL AND CONTROL GROUPS

Whereas in many experiments the various treatment groups consist of different levels of the independent variable (see examples above), there are other occasions in which an experimental group and a control group are used. Although these experiments can be described using the above definition of independent variable, a separate section is used to discuss these concepts because they present some unique problems of experimental design.

The experimental group of subjects is the group that receives the experimental treatment, that is, some manipulation by the experimenter. The control group is the group of subjects who are treated exactly like the experimental group except that they do not receive the experimental treatment. The Spallanzani experiment is a good example of this. The group of bitches receiving the sperm-free filtrate was the experimental group and the group receiving the normal semen was the control group.

EXAMPLE

Blind persons are very adept at avoiding obstacles; however, little was known as to how they do this. One theory was that blind people have developed a "facial vision", i.e., they react to air pressure on exposed surfaces of the skin. A second theory was that avoidance of obstacles comes through the use of auditory (hearing) cues. Supa, Cotzin, and Dallenbach (1944) set out to test these theories. They had blind people walk around in a large room in which obstacles (screens) had been set up. Two experimental treatments were used. In the first treatment, blind subjects wore a felt veil over their face and gloves on their hands (thus eliminating "skin perception"). In the second treatment, blind subjects wore ear plugs (thus eliminating auditory cues). A third treatment was the control treatment in which blind subjects walked around the room as they would normally. The results indicated that subjects in the control and in the felt-veil treatment avoided the obstacles every time, but the subjects in the ear-plug treatment bumped into the obstacles every time. Based on these results the authors concluded that the adeptness of the blind in avoiding obstacles is due primarily to their use of auditory cues and not due to any "facial vision."

The above experiment is an abbreviated version of a series of experiments on the perception of normal and blind subjects. In this example, it is difficult to specify an independent variable. The experiment is most easily described as having two treatment groups—one in which "facial vision" is eliminated and one in which auditory cues are eliminated. The control group is treated the same as the other treatment groups except they do not receive the precise treatment. The control group provides a "normal" baseline in order to determine whether the treatments improve or hamper the avoidance of obstacles. The dependent variable in this study was the number of times the subjects walked into the obstacles.

Sometimes more than one control group is needed. For example, in pharmacology a *placebo* control group is frequently used. A placebo group is best described as a group of subjects who are told that they are getting a treatment that will improve their performance or cure some symptom but actually are not. This type of control group is also used in testing the effectiveness of therapy.

EXAMPLE

Paul (1966) conducted an experiment to test the effectiveness of two types of therapy in treating "speech phobia." His subjects were students enrolled in public speaking classes at a large university. Paul took 67 students who had serious performance problems in the course (speech phobia) and assigned them to one of four conditions. One group of 15 subjects received a form of behavior therapy. A second group of 15 subjects received an insight therapy. A third group of 15 subjects received a placebo condition in which they were given harmless and ineffective pills and were told that this would "cure" them of their problems. A fourth group of 22 subjects was not given any treatment but simply answered questionnaires given to the other three groups. All subjects had to give a speech before the treatment began and one after the treatment had been completed. One dependent variable was the amount of improvement shown by the subjects from the first to the second speech based on ratings made by four clinical psychologists. These four psychologists were not involved in the therapy to the subjects nor did they know which subjects were in which treatment group. The results indicated that 100 percent of the behavior therapy subjects improved, 60 percent of the insight therapy subjects improved, 73 percent of the placebo subjects improved, and 32 percent of the no-treatment control subjects improved.

The Paul experiment illustrates the need (in some experiments) for different types of control groups. The interpretation of the results of the above experiment would have been quite different if Paul had not used a placebo control group. Without the placebo control group it would have appeared that insight therapy was actually effective (as a therapy) in improving speech difficulties. With the placebo group placed in the design it now appears that the insight therapy was not really effective as a therapy but may have only acted as a placebo itself. In fact, there was some tendency for the placebo group to improve more than the insight therapy group. The experiment also points out the need for a no-treatment control group. Over 30 percent of the subjects in this treatment improved in spite of the fact that they received no treatment, and this may form a baseline to measure the improvement rate if subjects are just left alone. Different types of control groups are used in different areas of research. In experiments in which animals are given operations and a part of the brain is removed, a control group is sometimes used which undergo all of the surgical procedures except that the brain is not tampered with. This would control for such factors as postoperative shock causing the effect found in the experimental group. The point to be remembered is that the control group is treated exactly like the experimental group except for the *specific* experimental treatment.

This experiment also illustrates an important control procedure that is used to avoid *experimenter bias*. The psychologists who rated the subjects' speaking performances were not the same people who treated the subjects in therapy nor did they know which subjects were in which experimental group. It is reasonable to assume that therapists might be biased (or defensive!) when it comes to judging the improvement of their own patients. Furthermore, the four judges might have their favorite therapy and if they knew which subjects had received this therapy they might be prone to see more improvement for these subjects than for subjects in the other experimental conditions. Or perhaps the judges would have assumed that the subjects in the no-treatment control group could not have improved (because they received no treatment) and therefore would rate the performance of these subjects as very poor. Paul controlled for these potential biasing effects by using independent judges, as well as keeping the judges blind as to what experimental group a particular subject was in. The term *blind* is used in a special sense in experimental research. *Single blind* usually means that those researchers who are judging the performance or progress of the subjects are not informed as to which treatment groups the subjects were in and may not be informed as to the nature of the experiment. The *double blind* is frequently used in drug research. Using this latter procedure both the judges and the patients are kept blind as to the type of drug that is being used and the type of effect that can be expected from the drug.

The Two Meanings of Control

The preceding discussion on control groups and on single and double blinds points out that there are two uses of the word "control" and both are very important. In the first, and literal, sense the experimenter makes things happen when he wants them to happen. This is what was meant by control when it was stated that Spallanzani had control over the insemination process, i.e., he could control the contents of the seminal fluid. The manipulation or selection of independent variables are prime examples of this type of control. Another example comes from the study of factors controlling nest building in canaries. Under natural conditions, these birds do small amounts of nest building scattered over rather long periods of time. In order to study this behavior experimentally, it is necessary to get the birds to build during those times when the experimenter is prepared to make his observations. This problem is solved by keeping canaries in cages and giving the nest material only when the researcher is there to observe. Here the presentation of nest material has been controlled (manipulated) and precise observations of nest building behavior can be made.

The second use of the word control is in arranging conditions so that the experimenter can attribute the result to the independent variable and not to some other variable. Paul controlled for the judges' bias by keeping the judges blind. The use of "control groups" is an attempt to insure that the results are not due to some other variable. In the Paul experiment the placebo control group "controls" for placebo effects and the no-treatment control group controls for spontaneous remission. This second use of control will be discussed more fully in Chapter 3.

CURVES AND FUNCTIONS

Earlier, independent and dependent variables were discussed and in both of the examples cited we arrived at some general conclusions about the relationship between variables. In the first example it was concluded that spaced practice was superior to massed practice; in the second example it was concluded that the information given first about a person has more "weight" than information given later in forming an impression of that person. While these general conclusions are valuable, many psychologists strive for greater precision in determining the relationship between two variables. One way of accomplishing greater precision is to set up the experiment in a manner such that a curve can be drawn that illustrates the relationship between two variables. A curve can be drawn any time the experimenter has values for the dependent variable for several levels of some other variable (usually the independent variable). The plotting of curves allows the researcher to "see" fairly precisely the relationships between two variables. For example, the slopes or shapes of "learning" curves can be compared to determine more precisely the effect of certain types of reinforcement on conditioning. At a perhaps more sophisticated level, curves can be used to derive a mathematical equation that describes the relationship between two variables. This mathematical equation or *function* is simply a shorthand method of describing the relationship. Once the function is derived, all one has to do is plug in the value for one variable and with a few, usually simple, calculations he can find the value of the second variable.

Three examples are presented below. The first two are "classic" studies, one from the area of audition and one from the area of learning. To the best of the authors' knowledge, no functions have been fitted to the data from these studies. The third example is from the area of psychophysics and is an example of a fairly well-substantiated mathematical "law."

EXAMPLE

Several experiments in the area of audition have been conducted to determine the relationship between the frequency (pitch) of a tone (as measured in cycles per second) and a subject's sensitivity to the intensity of that tone. One procedure (Hirsh, 1966) for investigating this problem is to present a pure tone to the subject through earphones. The tone is presented at a clearly audible level and then the intensity (loudness) of the tone (as measured in decibels) is gradually decreased until the subject signals that he can no longer hear the tone. The point or decibel level at which this signal is given is called the *descending threshold*. The procedure is then reversed with the same tone being presented at an inaudible level and the intensity being gradually increased until the subject signals that he can hear the tone. The decibel level at which this signal is given is called the *ascending threshold*. This procedure is repeated several times for the same subject on the same tone.

The dependent variable is the *absolute threshold* for that particular tone, which is the decibel level above which the subject will hear the tone and below which he will not hear the tone. The absolute threshold for a given tone is determined by averaging the threshold values obtained in the descending and the ascending trials. For example, suppose a tone of 100 cycles per second is presented to a subject and the values of the descending threshold for three attempts were 40, 45, and 42 decibels. The values of the ascending threshold for three attempts were 48, 49, and 52 decibels. To get the absolute threshold we would sum the six values (sum = 276) and divide by the number of values (6) which would yield an absolute threshold of 46 decibels for that particular tone and for that particular subject.

After the absolute threshold of a tone of a given frequency is determined for a subject, the above procedure is repeated for a tone of another frequency. Once the absolute threshold for six or eight tones of varying frequencies has been ascertained, the experimenter can plot a curve. Fig. 2.1 has been constructed from data presented in Stevens and Davis (1938). In this example, four subjects were tested at 10 levels of frequency (25, 50, etc.).

The points on the curve are the mean *absolute threshold* values for the four subjects at each level. For example, at the level of 50 cycles per second the absolute threshold values for the four subjects were 59, 60, 63, and 66 decibels. To get the mean these four values are summed (sum = 248) and the sum is divided by the number of values (248 ÷ 4) which yields a mean of 62 decibels. This procedure is followed for each of the levels tested. The points are then connected to form a curve.

The results indicate that the subjects are rather insensitive to low pitch or low frequency tones. Sensitivity increases as frequency increases up to a point, with the subjects being most sensitive to tones that range between 1,000 and 3,000 cycles per second. Beyond that point, however, sensitivity decreases.

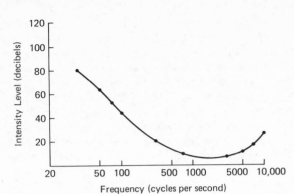

Fig. 2.1   The relationship between frequency and intensity on absolute auditory thresholds.

The independent variable in the above example is frequency as measured in cycles per second, and the dependent variable is the absolute threshold as measured on a decibel scale. In plotting a curve it is customary to place the values of the dependent variable on the vertical axis (the *ordinate*) and the values of the independent variable on the horizontal axis (the *abscissa*). The values of these two variables go from low to high as one goes out from the point at which the two axes intersect or meet. This procedure was followed in plotting the curve in the above example. The resulting curve quite clearly illustrates the relationship between the two variables.

The research strategy used here is sometimes referred to as *parameter estimation*, in contrast to *hypothesis testing*. The parameter testing research may not start out with some hypothesis to be tested but rather is an attempt to precisely measure the relationship between two variables. From a methodological viewpoint, however, there is little difference between this experiment and those described on p. 7. The experimenter manipulates the independent variable, measures its effects on the dependent variable, and holds all other variables at a constant level. The only difference is that the experimenter can accurately manipulate several levels of the independent variable, and because of this, he can determine fairly precisely the relationship between the independent and dependent variables.

In the above example, there were 10 levels of the independent variable (frequency) and each subject was tested at all 10 levels. The curve drawn in Fig. 2.1 connects the performance of subjects at each of the 10 levels. Another type of curve that is frequently encountered in psychological research is one in which each subject is tested at only one level of the independent variable; however, he is repeatedly tested at this level over a series of trials or time periods. The most common examples of these types of curves are found in experiments on learning in which the subject's improvement on a task is plotted as a function of the number of times he performs the task. The following example is a classic experiment in the field of learning and it illustrates the way in which such a "learning curve" is obtained.

EXAMPLE

Thorndike's Law of Effect stated that the connection between stimuli and instrumental responses are strengthened if the connection is followed by a satisfying state of affairs. For example, in the training of animals a command is given, the animal executes (or is shown how to execute) an instrumental act, and then the trainer rewards the animal with food or affection. The "satisfying state of affairs" (food or affection) strengthens the connection between the command and the instrumental act. A corollary to the Law of Effect postulated that large rewards produce stronger connections between stimuli and instrumental responses than do small rewards. This assumption was used to explain why animals learn more quickly (or at least show better performance) when they are given large rewards than when they are given small rewards. Elliott (1928) designed an experiment to test this assumption using a multiple-T maze. This maze is similar to that found in amusement parks or children's games, and it consists of a set of passageways constructed in the form of a series of T's. From the start box the rat goes down a runway at the end of which he must turn either left or right. One of these turns leads to a dead end, the other leads to another runway at the end of which it must again make a left or right turn. This process is continued for a series of T's and at the end of this series, the rat receives a food reward. Performance in the maze is determined by the number of errors (wrong turns) the rat makes during a trial. A trial begins when the rat leaves the start box and ends when the rat enters the goal box and receives the reward. Fig. 2.2 illustrates a multiple-T maze.

Two experimental groups (each consisting of 10 rats) were given one trial a day in the maze for a period of 16 days. One group of rats was given bran mash upon completion of the maze which may be considered a preferred (high value) reward for rats. The second group of rats was given a sunflower seed which has low reward value. The experimenter also carried out a second manipulation in that on the tenth trial the high

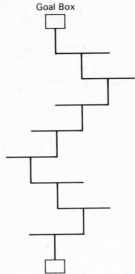

Goal Box

Fig. 2.2   A multiple-T maze.   Start Box

reward group was switched to the sunflower seed reward; however, the reward for the low reward group was not changed. The performance curves, as measured by the mean number of errors committed by each group on each trial, are shown in Fig. 2.3.

The figure indicates quite clearly that there is better performance (i.e., fewer errors) by the high reward group than by the low reward group, which supports the Law of Effect. However, after trial 10 this is suddenly reversed with the high reward group now making more errors than the low reward group even though the reward is exactly the same now for both groups. The Law of Effect would hypothesize that the high reward group would have developed stronger connections and consequently these animals should maintain higher performance even with a shift in reward. The results are in the exact opposite direction to that hypothesized from the Law of Effect and as such are rather serious evidence against the general law.

While this experiment is being used to demonstrate the use of curves, it has important theoretical implications. The reversal effect found in this experiment is now called the Crespi effect because Crespi (1942) conducted a rather systematic investigation of this phenomenon. The results seem to point out a difference between learning and performance. The magnitude of reward apparently

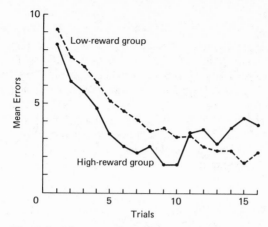

Fig. 2.3   Mean number of errors per trial.

affects performance and not learning. In the experiment reported above, it seems plausible that both groups learned the task equally well but the magnitude of reward effected how well they performed on the task. It should also be noted that while experiments of the type reported above have led to the rejection of Thorndike's Law of Effect as an explanation for learning, recent evidence (e.g., Bitterman, 1969) has suggested that the law may still be valid.

Curves such as those presented in the above example are frequently used in psychology. Whether they are called learning curves, conditioning curves, or performance curves the basic idea is the same. Subjects perform the same task over a series of trials and their performance across these trials is plotted. The dependent variable appears on the vertical axis of the figure and the time measure (e.g., trials) is placed on the horizontal axis. Separate curves are drawn for each independent variable treatment.

The performance curve shown in the previous example is descriptive. The data is presented in graphic form and this allows the reader to easily ''see'' how performance changes over a series of trials. At a more sophisticated level, curves can be used to derive a mathematical function or law that is predictive of the relationship between two variables. While there are few general mathematical laws in psychology, the experiment below is illustrative of one such law, the power law in psychophysics.

Psychophysics is defined as the branch of psychology which investigates the relationship between physical stimuli and sensory events. If a faint light is shined in your eye, you have a sensation of brightness. If the light is made stronger, the sensation becomes greater. It is evident that there is a relationship between the amount of light reaching to the eye and perceived brightness, and the exact nature of this relationship is one of the areas of study in the field of psychophysics. Stevens (1962) has suggested that there is a rather simple law relating the stimulus with the sensation. This law is called the *power law*. The power law relating the psychological magnitude ψ (psi) to the physical stimulus ϕ (phi) can be written

$$\psi = k(\phi_0 - \phi)^n$$

where ϕ_0 is the threshold value of the stimulus, i.e., point at which the subject "sees" the light. The ϕ value is the value of the stimulus being presented. The k is a constant that is determined by the choice of units and the exponent n varies with the stimulus modality, i.e., whether it is light, sound, etc.

Hilgard (1969) reported a test of the power law for the perception of pain. The technique used for manipulating pain was the *cold pressor test* in which the hand and forearm of a subject is placed in circulating cold water of a fixed temperature. In this experiment the hand and forearm were immersed in cold water for approximately 40 seconds. While the hand and forearm were immersed, the subject reported the pain he felt by calling out a number from 0 to 10. On the 0 to 10 scale, 0 represented no pain and 10 represented pain so severe that he wanted to remove his hand. The threshold for cold pressor pain is approximately 18 degrees Centigrade (i.e., that is the point at which subjects begin reporting pain) and Hilgard tested subjects under temperatures of 15°C, 10°C, 5°C, and 0°C. Between 9 and 23 subjects were tested at each temperature level.

The left side of Fig. 2.4 reports the mean pain for the four treatment groups and the right side reports the same means when logarithm scales are used for both temperature and pain.

It is evident from Fig. 2.4 (left) that with each succeeding increase in "coldness" (i.e., decrease in temperature) there tends to be less of an increase in reported pain—there is less of an increase in reported pain as temperature goes from 10° to 5° than when temperature goes from 15° to 10°. There is also less of an increase in reported pain when temperature goes from 5° to 0° than when temperature goes from 10° to 5°. There are two ways to test whether or not the power law fits these results. The easiest method is to plot the means on a figure, using a log scale for both the temperature and pain variable. If, using the log-log scale, a

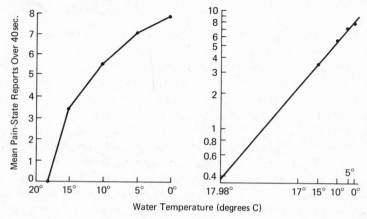

Fig. 2.4 The relationship between water temperature and reported pain-state. The two curves plot the same data, but the one on the right is based on a logarithmic scale.

linear (i.e., straight line) relationship exists between the two variables then the power law is supported. This procedure is presented in Fig. 2.4 (right) and shows strong support for the power law.

The second method of testing to see if the power law fits these results is to ascertain whether it is possible to find numerical values for k and n in the power law formula that will fit each of the points of the curve in Fig. 2.4 (left). If n is estimated to be .5 and k is estimated to be 1.92, the predicted values made by the power law show a good fit with the actual values shown in Fig. 2.4 (left). For example, to predict the pain level at 10°C:

$$\psi = k(\phi_0 - \phi)^n$$
$$= 1.92 \ (18 - 10)^{.50}$$
$$= 1.92 \ (8)^{.50}$$
$$= 1.92 \ (2.83)$$
$$= 5.4$$

This value of 5.4 approximates the value obtained in Fig. 2.4 (left). The power law shows as good a fit to the other three points of the curve.

The power law has been demonstrated to adequately handle a variety of psychophysical data. It has been shown to fit such diverse phenomena as brightness, loudness, severity of electric shock, apparent length of lines, weight, warmth, and cold. The study reported by Hilgard extends this list to include cold pressor pain. Thus there seems to be a rather simple psychophysical law relating physical stimuli to sensory events.

FACTORIAL DESIGNS

The experiments discussed so far manipulated only one variable. In the first example presented in this chapter, the single variable manipulated was the time between trials. In the second experiment presented, the single variable manipulated was the order of presentation of the adjectives. While such experiments are very important, it is evident that behavior is rarely a function of a single variable but rather is a function of several variables. For example, evidence from the field of developmental psychology indicates that if a child's parents are hostile and negative toward the child, as well as very controlling of his behavior, the child tends to become inactive and withdrawn. On the other hand, if the hostile and negative parental behavior is combined with a tendency to ignore the child and exert no control over his behavior, the child tends toward antisocial behaviors. These two variables, (1) degree of love—hostility, and (2) degree of control, both seem to be quite important in determining the child's behavior.

In order to determine the influence of two or more independent variables on the dependent variable, researchers employ a *factorial design*. In a factorial design two or more variables are manipulated at the same time. To illustrate this design consider the earlier experiment which involved the performance of rats under high and low reward conditions. The independent variable was the magnitude of reward. This design can be extended by manipulating another variable—the amount of food deprivation—as well as the magnitude of reward in order to examine the effects of both variables on performance.

EXAMPLE

Ehrenfreund and Badia (1962) examined the performance of rats under high and low food deprivation conditions, and high and low incentive conditions. The apparatus used in the experiment was a straight alley, 5 feet long. The alley contained a start box on one end and a goal box on the other end. The dependent variable was the speed at which the rats ran down the alley. Twenty rats were used in this experiment. During the experiment half of the 20 rats were maintained at 95 percent of their *ad lib* or free-feeding weight and the other half were maintained at 85 percent of their ad lib weight. (Ad lib or free-feeding weight is the weight of the rat when it is allowed to eat as much food as it wants.) For purposes of this experiment the high food deprivation treatment was defined as those rats maintained on 85 percent of ad lib weight, and low food deprivation treatment was defined as those rats maintained on 95 percent of their ad lib weight.

One-half of the rats in the high deprivation treatment received a 45 milligram (mg.) food pellet (low incentive) in the goal box, and the other half of the rats received a 260 mg. food pellet (high incentive) in the goal box. Combining the incentive treatments with the deprivation treatments yields the four experimental treatments of the experiment:

1. High deprivation — High incentive
2. High deprivation — Low incentive
3. Low deprivation — High incentive
4. Low deprivation — Low incentive

There were five rats in each of these four conditions.

Performance was measured in terms of the speed at which the rats transversed the middle 2-foot section of the runway. In the analysis presented here the authors took the median running speed for each rat on the last 10 trials of the experiment. Each rat's median score was converted to its reciprocal by dividing each score into 10. The conversion to reciprocals simply changes the direction of the scoring such that the higher the score, the faster the rat is running. The means of the reciprocal scores for each of the four treatment groups is presented in Table 2.1.

Table 2.1 Mean Running Scores for Deprivation and Incentive Groups

		BODY WEIGHT	
		95%	85%
Reward	45 mg.	10.26	13.92
	260 mg.	13.86	15.15

It is evident from means that both deprivation and incentive are influential in determining performance. The means for the high reward groups (260 mg.) are higher than the means for the low reward groups, within each deprivation level. Further, both of the means for the high deprivation groups (85 percent body weight) are higher than the means for the low deprivation groups.

The preceding example is called a 2 × 2 factorial design. There are two levels of one variable (deprivation) which are combined factorially with two levels of a second variable (incentive) to yield 2 × 2 or four separate treatments. Each level of the first variable occurs within each level on the second variable, i.e., high and low incentive is tested both under high deprivation and under low deprivation conditions. The design can be extended to add other variables; for example, a 2 × 2 × 3 design would consist of two levels of the first variable, two levels of the second variable, and three levels of a third variable. In this latter design there would be 12 separate treatments. One of the advantages of the factorial design is that it allows the researcher to ascertain how variables combine with one another to determine the values on the dependent variable. The experiment presented below is a 2 × 2 factorial design which illustrates the power of such a design to pick out interactions between variables.

EXAMPLE

Several studies have shown that if a person is somehow induced to argue for an attitude position that he is opposed to, the more he is paid for the task, the more he changes his own attitude toward this attitude position. This result is consistent with a reinforcement explanation, i.e., money is a reward and the more money that is paid for arguing for an opposing attitude position, the more that position is "reinforced." On the other hand, several other studies have found the exact opposite effect. These studies support a dissonance theory (Festinger, 1957) explanation. This explanation assumes that dissonance (or a state of discomfort) is aroused when a person argues for a position he actually opposes. Furthermore, the smaller the amount of money given for doing this task, the greater the amount of dissonance that should be aroused since low sums of money provide inadequate justification for defending something to which a person is opposed. In order to relieve the dissonance the person should "convince himself" that he really is for the argued position. Therefore more attitude change would occur in the high dissonance (low money) condition than in the low dissonance (high money) condition.

In an attempt to resolve the conflicting results reported above, Linder, Cooper, and Jones (1967) hypothesized that the reinforcement hypothesis would be verified when subjects have no choice in arguing for the position they opposed. These researchers further assumed that the dissonance hypothesis would be supported under conditions when the subject somehow chose to argue for the opposed position. The logic for these hypotheses was based on the assumption that dissonance can only be created when a person chooses to do something he opposes but not when he is "forced" to do it.

The design used in this experiment was a 2 × 2 factorial design.

Subjects were college students who wrote an essay supporting a speaker ban law for colleges (which was a position they were against). The subjects either were simply told to write the essay (no-choice condition) or were given a choice as to whether or not they would write the essay (free-choice condition). In addition, half of the subjects in each of the above two conditions were paid $.50 for writing the essay, while the other half of the subjects were paid $2.50. Thus, the design consists of the 4 treatments, and 10 different subjects were randomly assigned to be in each of the four treatments. The dependent variable was the amount of change in the subjects' attitudes toward the speaker ban law. This was measured by having the subjects check the point on a scale which indicated the degree to which they approved of the speaker ban law. The mean scale point attitude change for the four treatments is given in Table 2.2.

Table 2.2   Mean Attitude Change for Choice and Incentive Conditions

| | | INCENTIVE | |
		$.50 INCENTIVE	$2.50 INCENTIVE
Choice	No-choice treatment	− .05	+ .63
	Free-choice treatment	+ 1.25	− .07

Positive scores indicate change toward the position argued in the essay (for a speaker ban law), while negative scores indicate change against the argued position (a "boomerang" effect). The results support the authors' hypothesis. In the no-choice treatment, the $2.50 incentive elicited more attitude change than did the $.50 incentive. In the free-choice treatment, the opposite result was found.

The appropriate statistical test to analyze the above results is *analysis of variance*. The actual calculations of this statistic will not be explained here. However, some of the logic of this test will be described because it gives some insight as to the logic of a factorial design as well as to point out how the results are analyzed. The basic design was a 2 × 2 factorial design with two levels of one variable (no-choice or free-choice) and two levels of a second variable ($.50 incentive or $2.50 incentive). In the analysis of variance each factor (or variable) is analyzed separately and then the interactions between these variables are analyzed. In the example-experiment above there are two factors, therefore the analysis of variance will contain (1) an analysis of the *main effect* of the first variable, (2) an analysis of the *main effect* of the second variable, and (3) an analysis of the *interaction* between the two variables.

The main effect of the choice variable is analyzed by comparing the mean attitude change of subjects in the no-choice condition versus subjects in the free-choice, ignoring the incentive manipulations. The mean of the no-choice condition is calculated by adding the means for both incentive conditions and dividing by two ($-.05$ plus $+.63 = +.58$, $+.58$ divided by 2 $= +.29$). The same process is done in the free-choice condition with a resulting mean value of $+.59$. These two means are then compared ($+.29$ versus $+.59$) in order to analyze for the main effect of choice. The same process is repeated in order to analyze the main effect of incentive. By doing the necessary addition and division, it is found that the mean attitude change for the $.50 condition is $+.60$ and the mean for the $2.50 condition is $+.28$. These two means are then compared to ascertain the main effect of incentive. The next step is to analyze the interaction effect. The test for an interaction effect is a test to determine if the two variables are independent of one another with respect to their influence on the dependent variable. The variables are nonindependent (and interact) if it is demonstrated that the one variable shows a different pattern of results under each of the two levels of the second variable. In a 2 × 2 design the test for the interaction effect can be made by adding the means in the diagonal cells of Table 2.2 and dividing by two. Thus the mean for the no-choice $.50 condition is added to the high-choice $2.50 condition ($-.05$ plus $-.07$ divided by 2 $= -.06$). The same process is repeated on the other diagonal means ($+.63$ plus $+ 1.25$ divided by 2 $= +.94$). These two means ($-.06$ and $+.94$) are then compared to determine the interaction effect.

Linder, Cooper, and Jones analyzed their results in a manner as described above. Their computations indicated that although there were differences in the mean attitude change both for the main effect of choice and for the main effect of incentive, these differences were not *statistically significant*. That is to say, the magnitude of these differences was not greater than what would be expected by a chance fluctuation in the means. The interaction effect was found to be statistically significant in the direction hypothesized by the authors—high incentive facilitates attitude change in the no-choice condition, but low incentive facilitates attitude change in the free-choice condition. Thus the two variables interact with each other to determine the amount of attitude change.

The 2 × 2 design is the simplest of factorial designs. These designs become increasingly complex as more factors are added, or when several levels of factors are used. The example below is illustrative of this point. Only two factors are used, with two levels of one factor and four levels of the second factor. This example was taken from research in educational psychology.

EXAMPLE

Much of the evaluation of learning in the classroom takes place via tests, quizzes, or papers. Quite frequently a student takes the test or turns in a paper on one day and it is returned several days later. In this situation there is *delayed information feedback*, i.e., there is a time delay between the student's taking of the test and his receiving information as to where he was correct and where he made his mistakes. This delayed feedback has been criticized as being poor educational procedure. Some new methods, such as programmed textbooks and teaching machines make use of an immediate feedback technique in that the student gives an answer to a particular question and finds out immediately whether he is right or wrong.

More (1969) designed an experiment to compare the effects of immediate and delayed feedback using verbal learning materials similar to those used in the school classroom. The subjects were eighth-grade students in four junior high schools. The material to be learned was the science information contained in a 1,200 word article on glaciers. The student read the article and was immediately tested on its contents by a 20 question multiple-choice test.

To test for the effects of delay of information, a 4 × 2 factorial design was used. The first variable was the length of delay between the taking of the test and the feedback as to the correct answers. There were four time intervals. One group received this feedback immediately as they answered each question on the test. The other three groups received the feedback either $2\frac{1}{2}$ hours, 1 day, or 4 days after taking the test. After the students received this feedback, they took the same test again. At this point the experimenter introduced the second variable, i.e., the student took the test immediately after receiving the feedback (acquisition treatment), or three days after receiving the feedback (retention treatment). The dependent variable was the number of questions (out of a possible 20) that were answered correctly by the student on the second administration of the test.

To summarize the procedure, the students read an article on glaciers and were immediately tested on this material. They then received feedback as to the correct answers after one of four time delays. They were then retested on the same test immediately after feedback or three days after feedback. There were three different classrooms of students in each of the eight treatment groups. The mean number of questions correct on the second test for each of the eight groups is given in Table 2.3. The results indicated that performance was higher in the acquisition group than in the retention group. This was expected as some forgetting would occur after three days. For the acquisition treatment it was found that the no-delay feedback group scored significantly lower on performance than the other three feedback groups. These latter three did not differ significantly from each other. For the retention treatment, the $2\frac{1}{2}$-hour and the 1-day delay groups scored significantly higher than either the no-delay or the 4-day delay groups. No significant difference was found between the $2\frac{1}{2}$-hour and the 1-day groups, or between the no-delay and the 4-day groups.

Table 2.3 Mean Second Test Performance of Treatment Groups

	DELAY OF FEEDBACK			
	NO DELAY	$2\frac{1}{2}$-HOUR DELAY	1-DAY DELAY	4-DAY DELAY
Acquisition treatment	15.1	16.7	16.9	16.7
Retention treatment	13.0	15.4	16.0	14.6

The author concluded that the results offer no support for the assumption that immediate feedback maximizes learning of the specific materials used in his study. Quite the contrary, delayed feedback of $2\frac{1}{2}$ hours or more produced superior learning in the acquisition treatment. For the retention treatment some, but not too much, delay maximizes the students' retention of the materials at a later date. The author felt that this latter finding was especially important since one primary objective of instruction is to maximize retention of material.

Most researchers find it valuable to draw a figure of the results of a factorial design since it enables them to "see" the relationship between the variables more clearly. Fig. 2.5 illustrates the results of More's experiment.

The dependent variable is on the vertical axis and one independent variable is on the horizontal axis. Separate curves are

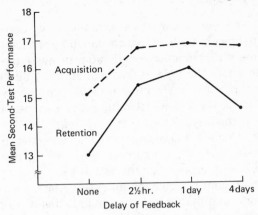

Fig. 2.5   Mean second test performance for acquisition and retention conditions.

drawn for each level of the second independent variable. The effects of delay in the experiment are more cearly illustrated by this figure. This experiment points out the possible complexity of the factorial design as well the value of having several levels of the factors. If only two levels of the delay factor had been used, the interpretation of the results for the retention treatment would have been quite different regardless of which two delay levels had been picked.

FUNCTIONAL DESIGNS

In the previously discussed research strategies the usual procedure was to assign several subjects to each experimental treatment. The mean (or percent) of the subjects' scores on the dependent variable were then compared with one another using the appropriate statistical test. While this procedure is common, a different research strategy is frequently used by those researchers who are interested in what they have called "the experimental analysis of behavior." This area of research originated with B. F. Skinner and workers in this area are sometimes called "Skinnerians." It is not entirely clear what label should be placed on the type of design frequently used in this area. The design has been called a *functional design* because of the use of functional definitions of terms and concepts in this area. A functional definition of a concept (e.g., punishment) is accomplished by specifying the relationship between a set of determining conditions and their effects on behavior, both of which can be precisely measured. The requirement that functional definitions be used to some extent leads one to adopt the type of research strategy described here.

In contrasting this research strategy with those previously discussed in this book, several differences can be noted. First, researchers in this area tend to be *atheoretical* in the sense that they are more concerned with examining variables that control behavior than they are concerned with testing some theory. Instead of viewing an experiment as a means of theory testing, variables which control behavior are systematically explored with the assumption that theory will emerge inductively from the data. A second difference is that researchers in this area will commonly use only one or two subjects rather than large groups of subjects in each experimental treatment. Many observations are taken on a single animal as opposed to a single observation on many animals. The regularity of response caused by a particular stimulus condition is demonstrated for a single subject. These researchers also tend to report their data in the form of a "typical" response curve instead of comparing means (and variances) of several treatment groups. A typical response curve is a segment of the subject's behavior that is deemed typical of his performance under the particular experimental conditions. Another difference is that a statistical analysis of the data is not used but the typical curve (or curves) is presented for "visual inspection" of the regularities in response that are representative of that particular stimulus condition.

Researchers in this area commonly use a highly controlled experimental situation. For example, an animal is placed in a Skinner box, a chamber which typically contains only a bar to be pressed by the animal, a food dispenser, and some signal lights. In this simple situation, numerous independent variables can be manipulated such as the particular *schedule* of reinforcement under which the food is dispensed. For example, the reinforcement may be dispensed on a *fixed-ratio schedule* in which the animal is reinforced with a food pellet after it presses the bar a fixed number of times (e.g., 1, 16, 47, or 100). In another reinforcement schedule (*fixed-interval schedule*) the animal receives a food pellet for pressing the bar at least once in every fixed time period (e.g., 30 seconds or 4 minutes) regardless of the animal's activity within that time period. The dependent variable in the above cases is the frequency of bar pressing responses and is usually presented in the form of a *cumulative frequency* curve. The example below is illustrative of research using this strategy and was taken from Ferster and Perrott (1968).

The apparatus used in this experiment was a Skinner box. This box is approximately 14 inches square. The only contents of the box are a small plexiglas plate on one wall and a food magazine on the same wall. The plate and food magazine are connected such that if the plate is pushed, a food pellet will be released from the food magazine. Both the plate and the releaser mechanism are attached to a cumulative recorder. The recorder consists of a pen which is mounted on a sliding arm. The pen point rests on a strip of paper which passes slowly over a cylinder with the passage of time. If no responses are made by the animal, the pen point merely leaves a straight line as the paper passes over the cylinder. Each time the pigeon pecks the plexiglas plate the pen moves a small step in one direction on the paper and does not return to its original position. When the paper is examined, it is rather easy to see the animal's rate of response by noting the rate at which the pen moved (upward) in a given time period.

The subject used in this experiment was a pigeon who had previous experience with this apparatus. The pigeon was kept at 80 percent of its free-feeding body weight throughout the experiment, i.e., 80 percent of the weight it maintained when it was allowed to eat all that it wanted. The pigeon was placed in the Skinner box for one hour per day over a six-week time period. In the box the pigeon was reinforced for pecking the plate on a *fixed-ratio schedule*, i.e., the pigeon received a food pellet after pecking the plate a fixed number of times. Several fixed-ratio values were used. During the first week the pigeon received a food pellet after 70 pecks (FR 70), during the second week, a food pellet was received after 185 pecks (FR 185); and during the third week, the food pellet was received after 325 pecks (FR 325). The order was then reversed for the next three weeks.

Fig. 2.6 shows the performance at each of the three fixed-ratio schedules. Each segment is an excerpt which is typical of the pigeon's daily performance on each schedule. The dots indicate the point at which reinforcement was delivered. The rate of performance in each segment can be estimated by comparing the overall slope of each segment with the slopes given in the grid in the lower right-hand corner of the figure. The slope indicates that when the pigeon was responding, it responded approximately 3 or 4 pecks per second. When 70 pecks are required

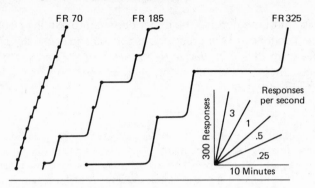

Fig. 2.6   Rate of responding under three fixed-ratio schedules.

for reinforcement, the bird's pecking is almost continuous with a very slight pause after each reinforcement. For FR 185 there is a longer pause after each reinforcement; however, when the pigeon begins pecking again, it starts at a very rapid rate which it maintains until the next reinforcement. The pause becomes much longer for FR 325; however, once the pigeon begins pecking again, it does so at the same rate that was noted for FR 70 and FR 185. The experiment indicates the number of pecks necessary for reinforcement does not affect the rate of pecking but has its influence on the length of pause between the dispensing of a reinforcement and the resumption of pecking.

This example illustrates the design strategy used in this area. A single subject was used who participated in three experimental conditions (i.e., three different fixed-ratio schedules). The data are presented in terms of "typical" response curves which indicate the regularities of response under the three conditions. No statistics are used. The experimental situation itself is highly controlled with precise measurement of the reinforcement conditions and the pecking responses. This same design has been applied to a variety of subjects and experimental situations. The example below is an application of the same strategy in an experiment designed to control abnormal behavior in a chronic schizophrenic.

EXAMPLE

The strength of a response may decrease as a function of continued reinforcement. This phenomenon is called *satiation*. It can be easily demonstrated in the laboratory situation by giving the animal continuous forcement is given over a long period of time, the animal will stop emitting the reinforced response. Ayllon (1963) used the satiation procedure to control hoarding behavior in a psychiatric patient. The subject was a 47-year-old patient in a mental hospital who collected towels and stored them in her room. Although the nurses repeatedly retrieved the towels, the subject collected more towels, and had an average of 20 towels in her room on any given day. Ayllon's procedure was to first establish a baseline as to the average number of towels in the subject's room under these "normal" conditions. After a seven-week observation period, a "reinforcement" period began. In this "reinforcement" or satiation period the nurses no longer removed towels from the subject's room. Instead they began bringing towels into the room and simply handing these to her without comment. During this period the number of towels brought into the room was increased from seven towels per day during the first week to 60 towels per day during the third week. The satiation period lasted for five weeks until the subject had accumulated 625 towels and had begun to remove the towels.

Fig. 2.7 reports the mean number of towels per week in the patient's

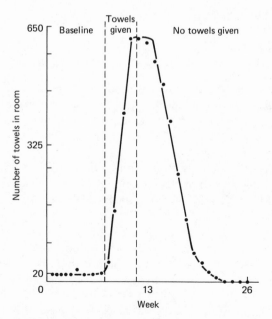

Fig. 2.7 Number of towels in patient's room prior to, during, and after treatment.

room over the period of the experiment. Note that this is *not* a cumulative record. After the satiation period the subject continued to remove towels from her room until at the twenty-second week there was an average of 1.5 towels in the room. This average continued through the twenty-sixth week. Ayllon made periodic observations throughout the next year and found that this average continued. The subject never returned to towel hoarding behavior nor did any other problem behavior replace it.

While the Ayllon experiment is an interesting demonstration of a "cure" for hoarding behavior, one should not lose sight of the fact that it is also a nicely controlled experiment using a functional design. Ayllon (1) establishes a baseline for the frequency of this behavior, (2) institutes a well-designed experimental treatment, (3) terminates the experimental treatment, and (4) continues observation of the frequency of the behavior over an extended time period. A single subject is used and no statistics are used. A point to be emphasized here is that sound experimental design is necessary to ascertain the regularity of behavior, whether the subject be a pigeon or a mental patient, and whether the behavior be pecking or towel hoarding.[1]

ADDITIONAL CONSIDERATIONS

The chapter has been concerned with some types of experimental designs used in psychology. While the basic logic of design is rather simple, the design and procedure may become fairly complex as has been seen in the case of factorial designs and as will be seen in the following chapters.

There are two points that need to be introduced at this time. First, one decision that the experimenter makes is how to operationally define his variables. Researchers usually have conceptual definitions of variables they wish to investigate. For example, psychologists talk about such things as anxiety, intelligence, ego-involvement, drive, distributed practice, and reinforcement; their theories are based on the relationships between concepts such as these. However, to do research, psychologists must some-

---

[1] For additional experiments, see T. Ayllon and N. H. Azrin. *The token economy: A motivational system for therapy and rehabilitation*. New York: Appleton-Century-Crofts, 1968.

how operationally define these concepts by specifying precisely how the concept is manipulated or measured. An operational definition is a statement of the operations necessary to produce and measure the concept. In the Elliot experiment (p. 17) the experimenter somehow had to operationally define high and low reward. Since Elliot had knowledge concerning what foods were preferred by rats, he could manipulate reward by using a highly preferred food substance (bran mash) as high reward and a low preference food substance (sunflower seed) as low reward. The dependent variable, performance, was defined operationally as the number of wrong turns in the multiple-T maze. Crespi (p. 18) performed an experiment to investigate the same general problem and he operationally defined high reward as 64 units of Purina Dog Chow and low reward as one unit of Purina Dog Chow. A unit was defined as one-fiftieth of a gram. The dependent variable was the time it took the rat to run down the straight alley, i.e., the time between the experimenter's opening of the start box and the rat's entering the goal box.

There is considerable variability as to the extent to which variables can be operationally defined in a manner that will be precise and that will retain the full meaning of concept that is being defined. On one hand, variables such as the spacing of practice as used in the Lorge experiment (p. 7), or the delay of feedback as used in More's experiment (p. 27), are fairly easy to operationally define. On the other hand, psychologists also use abstract concepts such as intelligence or anxiety which may be somewhat difficult to operationally define in a manner that includes the full complexity of that concept. Anxiety is a good example of such a variable. Almost everyone has some idea as to what "anxiety" is, and this concept is used by both psychologists and nonpsychologists. There are several dictionary definitions of this concept most of which agree that it is a complex emotional state with apprehension as its most prominent component. In attempting to operationally define this variable researchers have used pencil and paper tests, a palmar sweat technique, the galvanic skin response, heart rate, and eye movement. It seems probable that each of these operational definitions measures some part of this emotional state although none of them measures its total complexity. A researcher somehow must pick or develop an operational definition that is suited for his specific situation.

It is not within the scope of this book to conduct an extended discussion of conceptual and operational definitions; the interested reader will find a more thorough discussion in Underwood (1957). The concern here is that the reader be aware of the necessity to operationally define the variables used in research. Below are a series of abstract concepts used in psychology and it is suggested that the reader find operational definitions for these as part of a class exercise.

anxiety	ego-involvement	attitude
creativity	memory	punishment
aggression	learning	insight
intelligence	reinforcement	leadership
frustration	self-esteem	effort

The second point is that the experimenter is always confronted with the question as to how far he can *generalize* the results and conclusions of his experiment. In the Gordon Paul experiment reported earlier (showing the superiority of behavior therapy over insight therapy), there are several questions that can be raised concerning the generality of the findings:

1.   How far can the results be generalized across "illnesses"? Is behavior therapy superior only for speech phobia? Only for phobias in general? Only for "mild" mental problems including neurosis? Or is it superior for all mental problems?

2.   How far can the results be generalized across subjects? Are the findings only applicable to college students? Would the same results be found for children or for middle-aged persons? Would the same results be found for lower intelligence persons?

3.   Would the same results be found if the therapy time had been longer? Is behavior therapy effective as a "quick" therapy while insight therapy needs more time to produce its effects?

4.   Did improvement generalize to other situations? Was the improvement only for speech class situations, or all classroom situations, or all speaking situations?

There are several additional questions that could be raised, e.g.: Was the improvement temporary or permanent? However, the above four questions are sufficient to illustrate this point. The question of generalizability of results enters into all research and is not a criticism of the experiment. Rather it points out the limitations of a single experiment. In the single experiment, the researcher strives for tight control over his variables so that he can be fairly certain as to the validity of his results. In many cases this tight control is achieved by limiting the experiment to a specific behavior, to a specific sample of subjects, to a specific measurement technique, and to a specific time period. While these techniques of control are helpful (perhaps essential) in insuring the validity of the results found, they also raise questions of generality of the results. This is why one experiment leads to several other experiments making research an ongoing process with new problems to investigate and new knowledge to acquire.

DEFINITIONS

The following is a list of experimental design or procedure related concepts that were used in this chapter. Define each of these concepts:

independent variable
dependent variable
control group
placebo control group
subject variable
experimenter bias
experimenter blind
mean
operational definition
double blind

parameter estimation
generalization of results
ascending threshold
descending threshold
absolute threshold
conceptual definitions
factorial design
statistical interaction
massed practice
functional design

3

CONTROL OF EXTRANEOUS VARIABLES

TYPES OF CONTROL

The previous chapter focused on design strategies. In the examples given in the chapter, the experimenter *manipulated* some variable and observed the effect of this manipulated variable (i.e., the independent variable) on the dependent variable. The experimenter controlled the independent variable in the sense that he determined how much or what kind of the factor was presented. This is one form of experimental control. It was also emphasized that good design requires that the only variable manipulated is the independent variable and that *all other conditions are held constant* for the various treatment groups. "Holding all other conditions constant" is a second type of experimental control. If the various treatment and control groups are treated exactly alike *except* for the independent variable, then any differences observed on the dependent variable must be due to the independent variable. If some other (unwanted) variable is affecting the results, this variable is usually called an *extraneous variable* or a *confounding variable*. The variable is extraneous in the sense that it is an "extra" variable that has entered into the experiment. It is a confounding variable because the experimenter cannot be sure if the results he obtained are due to the independent variable or are due to the extraneous variable. Thus, the results of the experiment are inconclusive, and the experiment should be repeated using a design that eliminates the influence of the extraneous variable.

A variable is extraneous in a given experiment *only* when it can be assumed to influence the dependent variable. In an experiment in the area of learning, such variables as color of the subject's eyes, or height, or attitudes towards the United Nations probably have no effect on learning and the experimenter does not attempt to control these variables. On the other hand, there are variables such as motivation or intelligence that are known to affect learning, and these should be controlled for in a learning experiment. What variables are to be considered as extraneous (and therefore to be controlled) vary from experiment to experiment. Intelligence may be an extraneous variable in a learning experiment but may not be extraneous in an experiment to determine the absolute threshold of tones of varying frequencies. Thus the experimenter needs to control only a limited number of variables; those that can be assumed to influence the dependent variable.

This chapter is primarily concerned with the control of extraneous variables that occur when the experimenter manipulates the independent variable. That is, when the experimenter manipulates the independent variable is he also introducing, or failing to control for, an extraneous variable? A second group of related problems deals with insuring that the various treatment groups are equal as to subject characteristics. This will be discussed separately in Chapter 5 because a set of rather specific techniques has evolved to handle this problem.

Up to this point considerable emphasis has been placed on "holding all other conditions constant" as a means for controlling for the effects of extraneous variables. Actually this is only one of two very general techniques of extraneous variable control. A second method is through the use of treatment or control groups. All experiments use the first technique of control in that the experimenter attempts to manipulate only the independent variable. Some experiments also add treatment or control groups to further control extraneous variables. This latter technique is frequently used when the experimental manipulation itself may contain an extraneous variable as well as the independent variable. By adding treatment or control groups it then may be possible to separate the effects of the extraneous variable from that of the independent variable. These two techniques are discussed in more detail below.

Holding Conditions Constant

In the Lorge experiment on massed versus distributed practice (p. 7), the independent variable was the length of time between practice sessions. This was the only variable that was manipulated and all other variables appeared at the same level in all of the treatment groups. The same task was used for all treatment groups, all treatment groups had the same amount of practice, the task was such that it would be difficult for the treatment groups with spaced practice to rehearse in between practice sessions, the subjects were assigned to treatments such that the abilities of the subjects in each treatment were equal, etc. All of these factors could operate as extraneous variables, e.g., if one treatment group received more practice than another group, the results could be explained as being due to the amount of practice rather than to the spacing of practice. If the different treatment groups had performed different tasks, then the results could be explained as being caused by a difference in task variables (such as task difficulty) rather than in the spacing of practice. If the subjects in one treatment were better on task-related abilities than those in another treatment, then the results could be explained as being due to differences in the abilities in the treatment groups rather than to the spacing of practice. By insuring that these factors or variables were the same for all treatment groups, Lorge eliminated these variables as explanations for his results. This is the logic behind holding all conditions constant except the independent variable.

"Holding conditions constant" is obviously essential to good experimental design and this control strategy is easily understood by the beginning student of psychology. However, as will be seen in the following examples, even the most competent researchers may unknowingly violate this principle. While it is not possible to construct a checklist of extraneous variables (since they vary from situation to situation), there are some areas in which problems are especially prominent. For example, when the independent variable is a *subject variable*, i.e., a variable such as intelligence that the subject "carries around with him," there is always a danger that the subject variable manipulated is related in some systematic manner to another subject variable. If this is true then the results might be due to the second subject variable introduced inadvertently rather than to the one the experimenter manipulated. This problem is called a *subject variable—subject variable confound.* To illustrate this problem consider an experiment in which the researcher hypothesized that a person high on the personality trait of authoritarianism would have more difficulty learning complex material than a person low on this trait. This hypothesis was based on the assumption that high authoritarian persons think in a rather "simplistic" manner and therefore would have difficulty learning complex material. To test this hypothesis the experimenter had high authoritarian subjects and low authoritarian subjects learn some complex material. When tested for the recall of the material, the low authoritarian group showed considerably more learning than the high authoritarian group. One criticism of several leveled against this experiment was that it is well known that there is an inverse relationship between authoritarianism and intelligence—persons high on a measure of authoritarianism tend to be low on a measure of intelligence and vice versa. Therefore the fact that the high authoritarians learned less could be explained by the fact that they were less intelligent and the trait of authoritarianism had nothing to do with results. This criticism could be handled by matching the high and the low authoritarian groups on intelligence using a technique described in Chapter 5.

If a subject variable is not being manipulated, then a subject variable–subject variable confound is of little danger. However, the experimenter must be aware of other possible extraneous variables. Some of these problems will be discussed later.

Use of Treatment and Control Groups

This second technique for the control of extraneous variables has been briefly examined (see p. 10). Let us consider in more detail the Paul experiment (p. 11) on the treatment of speech phobia. The experimenter wanted to compare the effectiveness of two types of therapy. In addition, he had to consider what extraneous variables he would also be manipulating along with the therapy. If he was manipulating an extraneous variable along with the specific therapy, then any improvement might be attributed to the extraneous variable rather than to the therapy itself. There are two well-known extraneous variables which are present when a subject receives some sort of therapy. First, it is well established that some persons showing symptoms of some behavior problem will improve over time without receiving any specific treatment for this problem. This phenomena is called *spontaneous remission* because there is a disappearance of symptoms that appears "spontaneously," i.e., without any apparent treatment for the problem. In a therapy experiment the experimenter cannot be sure if the subject's improvement is due to the therapy itself or just due to spontaneous remission.

Secondly, it is known that some people who think they are receiving some established treatment for their problems (but actually are not) may show considerable improvement. This is called the placebo effect. The term comes from the Latin "to please," and the effect was discovered by physicians who would give patients some medically inert substance (e.g., sugar water) that resembles an active medication in order to please the patient rather than to provide physical benefit. Interestingly enough, it was discovered that some patients improved upon receiving placebo medication, especially those whose "illnesses" seemed to be psychosomatic. Since this placebo effect is assumed to occur in the treatment of psychological problems, any improvement in the therapy groups may be due to this effect rather than to the effect of the therapy itself.

To separate the amount of improvement due to spontaneous remission, due to the placebo effect, and due to the therapy itself, Paul used two control groups. Table 3.1 shows the four experimental groups as well as the variables influencing improvement in each of these groups.

Table 3.1   Variables Influencing Improvement in the Four Experimental Groups of the Paul Experiment

EXPERIMENTAL GROUPS	VARIABLES PRESENT INFLUENCING IMPROVEMENT			PERCENT IMPROVEMENT
	THERAPY	PLACEBO	SPONTANEOUS REMISSION	
1. Behavior therapy	Yes	Yes	Yes	100
2. Insight therapy	Yes	Yes	Yes	60
3. Placebo	No	Yes	Yes	73
4. No treatment	No	No	Yes	32

As indicated in the table, the experimenter can now separate the effects of the various variables that are influencing the subject's improvement. For example, we can subtract the amount of improvement shown in the placebo control group from the amount of improvement shown in each therapy group. This would give us an indication of the effectiveness of the therapy itself after we have eliminated the effect of the two extraneous variables.

Researchers will also frequently add treatment groups to the experimental design to insure that the results were not caused by an extraneous variable. Suppose that in the Asch study (p. 8) on impression formation he had only used a single treatment group that received the positive adjectives first and the negative adjectives last. With this single group the subject's evaluation of the person would be generally positive and this would support the hypothesis of a primacy effect in impression formation. If only this single treatment group was used in the experiment, several criticisms would arise. One criticism would be that Asch's negative adjectives were not really very negative and thus the person would have been evaluated positively regardless of the order of presenting the adjectives. Another criticism would be that people tend to evaluate other people positively regardless of what information is given. That is, people "look" for good traits in others and tend to like others. If this hypothesis is valid, then Asch would have gotten a positive evaluation of the stimulus person regardless of the order of presentation or regardless of the type of adjectives used. The experimental design used by Asch eliminated the above possible criticisms. One of his treatment groups received a positive to negative order of presentation of the adjectives. The second treatment group received a negative to positive presentation. The subject's evaluation of the person was positive in the first treatment and negative in the second treatment; therefore the above mentioned criticisms or explanations of the results are not valid. However, note that they are demonstrated to be invalid because Asch used two treatment groups instead of one.

It is difficult to formulate any specific principles about the control of extraneous variables. An experimenter usually begins with some problem to be solved or some hypothesis to be tested. In designing an experiment to test the hypothesis, he must keep in mind that he has to eliminate any extraneous variables that could be used as an explanation of the results. Certainly this would involve keeping all conditions constant except the independent variable, but it may also include the use of additional treatment or control groups. The best way for the student to learn what extraneous variables are to be controlled in any specific research area is to read experiments in this area. In this manner the student can become aware of the designs used by researchers in the area and also become aware of what variables have to be controlled for.

Some experiments which have appeared in the research literature involving control problems are presented below. The purpose of presenting these examples is not to criticize other researchers but to illustrate some problems that have arisen in the past. It is hoped that these examples will aid the student in analyzing a design for control problems.

CONTROL PROBLEM: SLEEP LEARNING

EXAMPLE

An experiment was conducted to determine if learning could take place during sleep. The material to be learned was the English equivalents of German words, and the subjects were 10 college students who reported that they had no knowledge of the German language. The subject slept in a comfortable bed in a sound-proof, air-conditioned laboratory room. The subject retired about midnight and at approximately 1:30 A.M. the experimenter entered the room and asked the subject if he was asleep. If there was no response, the experimenter turned on a recording that contained German words and their English equivalents, e.g., "ohne means without." There were 60 different words on the recording, and the record was played continuously until 4:30 A.M. If the subject awoke during the night, he was to call out to the experimenter and the recording would be stopped until the subject was asleep again. To test for learning, the 60 German words were played to the subjects in the morning and after each word the subject reported what he thought was the English equivalent of the word. The number of German words correctly identified was the dependent variable. The results indicated that the mean number of words correctly identified was nine (out of a possible 60), and the highest number correctly identified by any subject was 20. The experimenters interpreted these results as supporting the hypothesis that learning can occur during sleep.

This experiment has several important implications. At a theoretical level it suggests that during sleep the brain is actively processing information received by the external senses. At a practical level, it suggests that sleep learning may be an easy and effortless way to learn something. It should be a boon to college students who, instead of staying up all night to cram for an exam, can simply turn on a phonograph and go to sleep. While these results are quite exciting and one would like them to be valid, two major criticisms may be leveled against the experiment.

The first criticism was the failure to use a control group of subjects who had not been presented the learning material but who were given the recall test. While it is true that all subjects said that they had no knowledge of the German language, they may have been able to guess the meanings of some of the words. For example, Mann in German means man in English. Furthermore, some German words are frequently used in English particularly in old war movies, i.e., Schwein: pig; nein: no; ja: yes; etc. Thus, the apparent effects of sleep learning may actually be due to the subjects' ability to guess some words and some knowledge of other words, and a control group would have checked for this.

A second criticism dealt with experimenter's definition of sleep. Sleep was defined as what the subject did between 1:30 A.M. and 4:30 A.M. unless he reported that he was awake. On the other hand, it is known that there are various levels of sleep ranging from drowsiness to very deep sleep. It further is known that at drowsiness levels the subject has partial awareness of external stimuli; however, at the level at which sleep technically begins there is little or no awareness of external stimuli. In the experiment reported above there was no way of knowing what material was presented at what level of sleep. Therefore, it could be argued that any learning that occurred may have taken place at a drowsiness level rather than at a true sleep level.

Simon and Emmons (1956) designed an experiment to correct for the above problems. The materials to be learned consisted of 96 general information questions and their answers. They were presented in a question form, e.g., "In what kind of store did Ulysses S. Grant work before the war?" Then the answer was given: "Before the war, Ulysses S. Grant worked in a hardware store." Two groups of subjects were used: an experimental group who were given the answers to the questions while they were sleeping and a control group who simply took the learning test without having the answers played to them. To begin the experiment both groups were given the questions and asked to guess the answers. Those questions that the subjects answered correctly on this test were eliminated. Next, the experimental group was presented the questions and answers while they were asleep. During this period, recordings were made of their brain waves using an electroencephalograph (EEG). Because brain activity varies in a known manner at different stages of sleep, EEG records enable us to accurately determine the depth of sleep. As each answer was presented to the subject, the experimenter recorded the level of sleep of the subject. Thus, the experimenter had a record of the level of sleep at which each answer was given.

In the morning the experimental group was tested on the material that was presented to them during the night. This test was a multiple-choice test which consisted of the question plus five alternative answers. The subject was to guess which of the answers were correct. A multiple-choice test was used as it probably is a more sensitive measure of sleep learning in that the subject has only to recognize the correct answer rather than to recall it. The control group also took this test.

After the test scores were received, the experimenters separated the questions for each experimental subject into categories determined by the level of sleep at which the answer was played. The experimenters used eight levels of sleep which have been condensed into two categories for presentation below. Table 3.2 reports the percent of correct answers in these categories.

Table 3.2 Percent of Answers Correct at Three Sleep Levels

	LEVEL OF SLEEP		
	AWAKE	DROWSY	SLEEP
Experimental group	92%	65%	23%
Control group	24%	23%	23%

The data indicate that considerable learning took place when the experimental subjects were awake, and moderate learning appeared at a drowsy level. However, there was no apparent learning when the subjects were at a true sleep level. At this latter level the performance of the experimental group was the same as the control group subjects who had no learning experience. The 23 percent correct for the control group represents the number of correct answers that could be expected if subjects guessed which of the five alternative answers was correct.

In looking at the design of this experiment, it is important to note that the experimenters instituted several crucial control procedures to allow for a rather clear-cut test of sleep learning. First, to make sure that what appeared to be learned during sleep was not actually information that was previously known, the experimenters gave all subjects a pretreatment test on the material and eliminated the answers already known. Secondly, since a multiple-choice test was used as the test of learning, and since a certain proportion of the answers on such a test could be gotten correct by guessing, the experimenters used a control group to find out what the percent correct by guessing would be. Thirdly, the experimenters identified different levels of sleep and noted what answers were presented at each level. Using this technique it was possible to separate material presented when the subject was awake, was in a state of drowsiness, and was in a state of true sleep. Using these control procedures, the results suggest that no learning takes place at a true sleep level.

CONTROL PROBLEM: SOCIAL DEPRIVATION AND SOCIAL REINFORCEMENT

EXAMPLE

It has been repeatedly demonstrated that for animals who have been deprived of food, the effectiveness of a food pellet as a reinforcer is considerably enhanced. An experiment was conducted to determine if the same results would occur with social "deprivation" and social reinforcement in children. Subjects were 6-year-olds in an elementary school.

The effectiveness of social reinforcement was measured by a marble game. The game consisted of a box with two holes in it and the subject was to drop marbles one at a time into one of the two holes. For the first 4 minutes of the game the experimenter just watched the subject play the game. For the next 10 minutes the experimenter verbally reinforced the subject every time he put a marble in the hole that was least used in the initial 4-minute period. The verbal reinforcement consisted of the experimenter saying "Good" or "Fine" every time the subject put a marble in the "correct" hole. The dependent variable was the amount of increase in the subject's placing marbles in the "correct" hole from the 4-minute to the 10-minute reinforcement period.

In order to determine the effects of social deprivation the subjects were randomly assigned to one of three treatments. In the social *deprivation* treatment, the subjects were left alone in a room for 20 minutes prior to playing the game. In the *nondeprivation* treatment, the subjects started playing the game immediately after leaving their classroom. In the social *satiation* treatment, the subjects spent 20 minutes talking with the experimenter while they were drawing and cutting out pictures. This took place just prior to the game.

The results indicated that the subjects showed more of an increase in putting marbles in the "correct" hole in the deprivation treatment than in either of the other two treatments. Further, there was a greater increase in the nondeprivation treatment than in the satiation treatment. The results were interpreted as supporting the hypothesis that the effectiveness of social reinforcement is influenced by conditions of social satiation or deprivation in a manner similar to that found for food or water deprivation.

The above experiment has wide theoretical implications in that it has produced evidence to suggest that social drives seem to be subject to the same "laws" that have been established using the primary appetitive drives such as hunger. The authors also have developed a nice experimental situation to test this hypothesis since the experimental manipulations seem fairly clear cut and the dependent variable (i.e., the number of marbles in the "correct" hole) is easy to record without ambiguity. However, soon after the experiment was published, research critical of the experiment began to appear which argued that the results may have been caused by the failure to control extraneous variables.

One criticism of the experiment pointed out that when the experimenters were manipulating social deprivation ("social" being defined in terms of the amount of interaction with other people), they also manipulated general sensory deprivation. For example, in the deprivation treatment the child was not only isolated from other people but he also had no toys with which to play. In the satiation treatment the child not only interacted with the experimenter but he also drew and cut out pictures. Thus the experimenters comanipulated an extraneous variable (general sensory deprivation) along with social deprivation, and the results of the experiment might have been caused by this extraneous variable. Stevenson and Odom (1962) tested this alternative explanation of the results by comparing three groups of subjects. Before playing the marble game, one group of children was isolated and played with attractive toys for 15 minutes, one group was isolated for 15 minutes without toys, and a third group of children began playing the game immediately after being called out of the classroom. The results indicated no difference in the task performance of the two isolation groups but both groups had higher levels of performance (i.e., more marbles dropped in the "correct" hole) than the no isolation group. Since there was no difference in the task performance of the two isolation groups (both of which were socially deprived, but only one of which was deprived of toys), then the higher performance must have been due to the social deprivation. This supports the original interpretation of the experiment, and the influence of the extraneous variable was apparently very minor.

A second group of researchers raised a different criticism of the experiment. The crucial point of this criticism was that being placed in a strange environment by a strange adult should arouse anxiety in 6-year-olds. The greatest anxiety should occur in the deprivation treatment in which the subjects were left alone in a strange room for 20 minutes. The next highest level of anxiety should occur in the nondeprivation situation in which the subjects were led directly to the game situation. The least anxiety should occur in the satiation treatment because after 20 minutes of friendly conversation with the experimenter the subject should be somewhat comfortable in her presence. Since there is evidence demonstrating that heightened anxiety improves performance in some learning tasks (especially simple learning tasks), then the results of the experiment could be explained by the difference in anxiety arousal in the three treatments and there is no need to postulate some "social drive."

To test this hypothesis, Walters and Parke (1964) used a 2 × 2 factorial design in which they used two levels of isolation (either leaving the child alone for 10 minutes or starting the game immediately on coming from the classroom) and two levels of anxiety arousal. In the low anxiety condition the experimenter treated the subject in a pleasant and friendly manner, and in the high anxiety treatment the experimenter treated the subject in a rather cold and abrupt manner. Using these treatments: (a) no significant difference was found in performance between the two levels of isolation which is evidence against the social drive interpretation; (b) subjects in the high anxiety treatment performed better than subjects in the low anxiety treatment, which supports the anxiety arousal interpretation; and (c) the interaction effect was not significant. Thus it appears that an extraneous variable (arousal level) may have determined the results of the original experiment and the social deprivation interpretation may be invalid.

CONTROL PROBLEM: PERCEPTUAL DEFENSE

It has long been suggested that the human organism has certain mechanisms which protect it from anxiety provoking stimuli. One such mechanism is called *perceptual defense*. An experiment was designed to test the perceptual defense hypothesis by presenting to subjects neutral words and "taboo" words on a tachistoscope. This piece of equipment consists primarily of a shutter mechanism which can be manipulated so that a stimulus can be exposed to a subject for varying lengths of time. For example, the shutter can be adjusted so that the word is exposed for .01 of a second or for two minutes. The experimenter theorized that taboo words are anxiety provoking and while the subject may recognize them at an unconscious level a perceptual defense mechanism would delay the subjects recognition of them at a conscious level. Based on this assumption it was hypothesized that longer exposures would be necessary for the recognition of taboo words than for neutral words.

The subjects were eight male and eight female college students. Each subject was tested individually with both a male and a female experimenter present. Eleven neutral words (e.g., *apple, trade*) and seven taboo words (e.g., *whore, bitch*) were presented to each subject in a predetermined order. An ascending threshold method (see threshold discussion on p. 15) was used to determine the point at which the subject recognized the word. For each word the shutter was set at a very fast exposure speed (.01 of a second) and the exposure was gradually lengthened until the subject verbalized the word correctly. This process was repeated for each of the 18 words.

The mean threshold for the recognition of the neutral words was .053 seconds and the mean threshold for the recognition of the taboo words was .098. The difference between these two means was statistically significant. Since it took longer exposures (higher thresholds) for the subjects to recognize the taboo words than the neutral words, the experimenter concluded that the perceptual defense hypothesis was supported.

This experiment suggests that there is some process in the unconscious that determines whether a word is anxiety provoking, and if it is such, conscious recognition of the word is prevented or at least delayed. This is the notion of perceptual defense and it has far-reaching implications concerning human behavior.

It did not take long for other researchers to criticize the design. Howes and Solomon (1950) raised two methodological points.

First, they suggested that the results may be due to the subjects' reluctance to report a taboo word until they were absolutely positive of the identification of the word. The subjects might be particularly reluctant to verbalize these words in front of an experimenter of the opposite sex who was in the room. A second methodological point was that neutral words appear much more frequently in print than do the taboo words and therefore the subjects' quicker recognition of the neutral words was because they had seen these words more frequently. In a follow-up experiment Howes and Solomon (1951) demonstrated the validity of the "word-frequency" hypothesis. They obtained a listing of the frequency at which some 30,000 words appeared in print. They chose 60 words of varying frequencies (all nontaboo words) and determined the recognition thresholds of each word using a procedure similar to that used in the above example. They found a high negative correlation (approximately −.79) between the frequency at which the word appeared in print and its recognition threshold. That is, the more frequently the word appeared in print, the lower was its recognition threshold. While this experiment demonstrates that word frequency is a plausible explanation for results of the original experiment, it still can be argued that taboo words show a higher threshold even if frequency is controlled for.

Postman, Bronson, and Gropper (1952) made a more direct test of the word-frequency explanation by determining how frequently the taboo words appeared in print and matching them with neutral words that appeared in print at the same frequency. The list of words was presented to the subjects using a procedure similar to that of the above example. The results of this experiment indicated no support for the perceptual defense hypothesis. In fact (surprisingly enough), it was found that the recognition threshold for the taboo words was significantly lower than that of the neutral words. This was probably due to an underestimation of the frequency of the taboo words. Although research in this area continues, it appears that the early demonstration of the perceptual defense phenomenon may have been due to the confounding variable of word frequency.

CONTROL PROBLEM: ONE-TRIAL LEARNING

When a child is learning to read the alphabet he is shown the letters A, B, C, etc., while the teacher pronounces the name of the letters. This procedure is repeated until the child learns the association between the printed letter and the verbalized sound. There is a controversy among learning theorists as to whether this association is gradually built up (incremental process) or whether it occurs in an all-or-none fashion. The latter school of thought holds that if some learning trials have been given and the child is shown the letter and cannot verbalize its name then no association between the letter and its name has taken place. The former school of thought would argue that some association has taken place but this association is not yet at sufficient strength to allow the child to give the correct answer.

A rather ingenious experiment was performed to determine which of the above theories was correct. The task of the subjects was to learn eight nonsense syllable pairs. Each pair was presented to the subjects on a separate card. After the subject had seen all eight pairs he was then shown the first nonsense syllable of each of the pairs and asked to give the second nonsense syllable. This was the test of whether or not the pair had been learned. For example, one pair the subject was shown might have been POZ– LER. In the recall test the subject would be shown only the first syllable POZ, and he would have to supply the second syllable.

Two experimental groups were used. For the first experimental group the experimenter replaced every nonsense syllable pair that had not been learned on a single trial. For example, the subject was shown eight pairs and then given a learning test on these eight. Any pair that was not recalled was dropped out of the eight cards and a new pair was substituted into the list of eight. The eight cards (which now includes only pairs that were learned plus new pairs) are again shown to the subject and a recall test is given. The experimenter again eliminated those pairs that were not recalled and substituted new pairs. This process was repeated until the subject could recall all eight pairs given on a single trial. The second experimental group was treated like the first except that they were shown the same eight cards on each trial. Thus, eight pairs were shown, a recall test given, the same eight pairs shown, a recall test given, etc. This process was repeated until the subject could recall all eight of the pairs on a single trial.

The experimenter then compared the number of trials it took to learn all eight pairs in each treatment group. The mean number of trials for perfect recall for both groups was exactly the same (8.1). Since *all* pairs learned in the first experimental group were learned on one trial (or else they were thrown out), and since there was no difference in the number of trials necessary to learn the eight pairs perfectly in this condition from the one in which the same eight pairs were repeated, it was concluded that learning (i.e., associations) occurred in an all-or-none fashion. Stated a little differently, the experimenter argued that a gradual build-up of associations through repetition could have occurred in his second experimental group. If repetition is important in learning, then this second group should learn the eight pairs faster than the first group who learned eight pairs on a single trial without any repetition. Since there was no difference between the two groups, it was concluded that repetition is unnecessary for learning.

As might be expected, this experiment caused some excitement, particularly among those who support an incremental view of associative learning since the experiment suggests that this latter view of learning is invalid. It was not long after the experiment was published that research which criticized the experiment began appearing. One major criticism of the experiment was that the more difficult pairs were probably dropped out of the first treatment group and thus the final list learned by each subject in this treatment consisted only of the easier pairs. No pairs were dropped out of the second treatment group and thus the final list learned by these subjects consisted of both easy and difficult pairs. The failure of the experiment to find quicker learning in the treatment that involved repetition of the same pairs was due to the fact that the list learned by this group was more difficult than the final list learned by the subjects receiving the drop-out procedure.

In one test of the "item selection" hypothesis, Underwood, Rehula, and Keppel (1962) repeated the above procedure except that they added a control group who received lists composed of the pairs that subjects in the drop-out condition received on their last learning trial. Subjects in this condition were given the same word pairs on each trial. The results indicated that subjects in this latter condition learned all pairs in the list more rapidly than did those subjects given the list containing a random sample of all of the pairs used. Thus it appears that the subjects in the drop-out condition of the original experiment were learning easier pairs and this may be an explanation for the results.

SUMMARY

These four examples illustrate a variety of control problems. In the sleep learning experiment there was a failure to control for previous knowledge as well as level of sleep. In the social deprivation experiment there was a failure to separate social deprivation from sensory deprivation. Another criticism of this experiment was that results were due to arousal rather than to deprivation. In the perceptual defense experiment there was a failure to control for word frequency. In the one-trial learning experiment, the results were apparently due to the fact that the pairs learned in one treatment group were easier than those learned in the other treatment group.

The variety of control problems found in these examples illustrates why it is not possible to give the student a list of extraneous variables. Control problems vary so greatly from experiment to experiment, and from research area to research area, that no list is possible. To repeat an earlier statement, the student can best learn about experimental designs and control problems in a specific area of research by reading about experiments in that specific area. On the other hand, there are a variety of control problems that occasionally appear that are fairly easily recognized by the beginning student in psychology. The next chapter will allow the student to practice his knowledge on some of these problems.

DEFINITIONS

The following is a list of terms and concepts that were used in this chapter. Define each of the following.

extraneous variable	multiple-choice test
"holding conditions constant"	placebo effect
spontaneous remission	tachistoscope
electroencephalograph	recognition threshold

4

DESIGN CRITIQUES: I

On the following pages are a series of experiment "briefs." There is a design problem in each one of the briefs. The design problem occurs in the discrepancy between what the experimenter did in the experiment and the conclusion that he arrived at on the basis of the results. We have previously illustrated basic principles of experimental design. Now, the purpose is to expose you to a series of fictitious experiments and let you apply your knowledge of experimental design in critiqueing them. The use of the briefs is a quick way to expose you to a variety of problems in a variety of research areas. You do not need any expertise or technical knowledge in the research area being explored in the experiment; the problems can be recognized with a knowledge of design principles previously discussed in this text.

In criticizing the design of the experiment briefs, you should only make use of the information given in the brief. Do not criticize the design by inferring something that is not given. For example, if the experimenter used a pencil-and-paper anxiety test, you should assume that the test is valid and reliable unless information to the contrary is given. There is usually one major defect in each brief and you should concentrate your criticism on this major problem. Be specific as to the defect. For example, do not just say that the experimenter should have used a control group but point out exactly how this control group would be treated.

The following example illustrates how the briefs should be criticized:

A certain investigator hypothesized that the hippocampus (a part of the brain) is related to complex "thinking" processes but not to simple "thinking" processes. He removed the hippocampus from 20 rats. He had ten of the rats learn a very simple maze and had ten of the rats learn a very difficult and complex maze. The first group learned to run the maze without error within 10 trys (or trials). It took the second group at least 30 trials to run the maze without error. Based on these results, he felt his hypothesis had been confirmed—rats without a hippocampus have more trouble learning a complex task than they do learning a simple task.

In criticizing this design, it appears reasonable to assume that any rat would take more trials to learn a complex maze than it would to learn a simple maze. Thus the results found by the experimenter may have nothing to do with the removal of the hippocampus—rats with the hippocampus intact might show the same results. This criticism would suggest that in redesigning the experiment a 2 × 2 factorial design should be used. One factor is hippocampus intact or hippocampus removed. The second factor is simple or complex maze. This is diagrammed below:

	SIMPLE MAZE	COMPLEX MAZE
Hippocampus intact	10 rats	10 rats
Hippocampus removed	10 rats	10 rats

We would need a total of 40 rats with 10 rats being assigned to each of the four treatments. This revised design would allow for a more reasonable test of the experimenter's hypothesis than the original design. Although the redesign might become more complex than that noted above, this design is sufficient for the purposes of this book since it points out the major defect in the original experiment and indicates a way of correcting this defect.

EXPERIMENT BRIEFS

1.   An investigator attempted to ascertain the effects of hunger on aggression in cats. He took 10 cats, kept them in individual cages, and put them on a food deprivation schedule such that at the end of two weeks the cats weighed 80 percent of their normal body weight. He then put the cats together in pairs for 15 minutes and watched to see if aggression or fighting would occur. In *all* cases the cats showed the threat posture, and in most cases fighting occurred. The *E* concluded that hunger increases aggression in cats.

2.   An *E* wished to examine the effects of massed versus distributed practice on the learning of nonsense syllables. He used three treatment groups of *S*s. Group I practiced a 20 nonsense-syllable list for 30 minutes one day. Group II practiced the same list for 30 minutes per day

for two successive days. Group III practiced the same list for 30 minutes per day for three successive days. The E assessed each group's performance with a free recall test after each group had completed their designated number of sessions. The mean recall of the 20 syllables for Group I was 5.2; for Group II, 10.0; and for Group III, 14.6. These means were significantly different from one another, and the E concluded that distributed practice is much superior to massed practice.

3.   An investigation was undertaken to explore the hypothesis that females tend to react more to emotion whereas males tend to react more to rationality. The procedure used to test the hypothesis was an attitude change situation. The E presented an emotional communication on a specific social issue to 50 females and 50 males. Results indicated that females changed their attitudes (in the direction advocated in the communication) to a significantly greater degree than did the males. The E concluded that his hypothesis was supported.

4.   An experiment was designed to examine the relationship between drive and performance on a complex discrimination task. Drive level was measured by the Taylor Manifest Anxiety Scale. The top 15 percent of 300 subjects who took the test were designated as the High Drive group and the bottom 15 percent of the subjects were designated as the Low Drive group. These two groups of subjects performed the discrimination task and much to the experimenter's surprise there was no significant difference in the performance of the two groups. The E concluded that drive level does not affect performance on a complex discrimination task.

5.   An investigator set out to test the hypothesis that fear of punishment for poor performance has a detrimental rather than a facilitative effect on motor performance. As a measure of performance, the experimenter used a "steadiness" test in which the Ss task was to insert a stylus into a hole so that the stylus did not touch the sides of the hole. Each subject inserted the stylus in 15 different holes. The diameter of the holes was varied; in some cases the task was quite easy, and in some cases the task was quite difficult. The E manipulated fear by threatening the subjects with electric shock if they performed poorly on the task. He strapped an electric shock apparatus to the leg of each subject before he performed the task; however, he never shocked the subjects regardless of their performance. One group of subjects was threatened with 50 volts of electricity, and he called this his Mild Fear condition. A second group of subjects was threatened with 100 volts of electricity, and he called this treatment the High Fear condition. Contrary to his hypothesis, the High Fear subjects did not perform any worse than the Low Fear subjects—in fact, the means for both groups were approximately the

same. Based on these results, the E concluded that fear of punishment has little, if any, effect on motor performance.

6.   A certain psychologist was looking for the cause of college failure. He took a group of former students who had flunked out and a group that had received good grades. He gave both groups a self-esteem test and found the group that failed scored lower on the test than the college success group. He concluded that low self-esteem is one of the causes of college failure and further suggested that the low self-esteem person probably expects to fail and exhibits defeatist behavior in college—which eventually leads to his failure.

7.   An E took 20 Ss who said that they believed in astrology and gave them their horoscopes for the previous day and asked them how accurate the horoscope was in predicting the previous day's occurrences. The Ss indicated their opinion on a six-position scale that ranged from extremely accurate to extremely inaccurate. All 20 Ss reported their horoscopes as being accurate to some degree, and none reported his horoscope to be inaccurate. The E concluded that horoscopes are accurate.

8.   A 2 × 3 factorial design was used to evaluate the effect of dosage level of an experimental drug (Remoh) on the treatment of schizophrenia. Two patient classifications were used: (a) new admissions to a particular mental hospital, and (b) patients who had been institutionalized for at least two years at that hospital. Patients received one of three levels of dosage, either 3 grams per day, 6 grams per day, or 9 grams per day. There were 20 patients in each of the six groups. In addition to administering the drug, the experimenters also rated each patient each week as to the presence or absence of schizophrenic symptoms. After two months, it was found that very few (5 to 10 percent) of the long-term patients had improved regardless of dosage level. It was also found that approximately 50 percent of the newly arrived patients had improved in each of the three dosage level groups. The researchers concluded that (a) Remoh is effective only for new arrivals and not for chronic cases, and (b) a dosage of 3 grams per day is sufficient to maximize the effectiveness of this drug.

5

CONTROL OF SUBJECT VARIABLES

EQUALITY OF SUBJECTS IN TREATMENT GROUPS

In *all* psychological experiments the behavior of some species of animal is the focus of research. Since all psychological research uses subjects (human or otherwise), it is not surprising that psychologists have devoted considerable attention to solving the problems of the control of those extraneous variables that are due to the characteristics of subjects. In fact, a set of specific techniques has evolved that are applicable to a wide variety of research situations. This chapter will discuss the essential features of these techniques.

In research, the performance of one treatment group is often compared with that of another group. These groups consist of subjects who differ on a variety of traits which could influence the results. It is important that all treatment groups of an experiment are approximately equal as to these various traits so that whatever results are found are attributable to the independent variable and not attributable to the fact that subjects in one treatment were different on some trait (e.g., IQ) from subjects in another treatment.

Field studies provide the greatest possibility that the results are caused by subject differences rather than by treatment differences. In fact, in any study in which subjects are used in their natural groups, or have volunteered specifically for one treatment or another, the first question one should ask is how do the subjects in the various treatments differ. For example, a large manufacturing company held leadership training courses for lower-level employees. These courses were run on a volunteer basis and took place at night on the employee's own time. In evaluating the effectiveness of this course 10 years later, it was found that those persons who had taken the course had advanced further in the company than those who had not taken the course. While this result was interpreted as supporting the effectiveness of the course, an alternative explanation would be that the course may have attracted only those men who were highly motivated to advance in the company. Thus the "treatment" group may have consisted of highly motivated men, and the "control" group may have consisted of unmotivated men. If this explanation is valid, then the course may have had no effect at all; the results may simply be due to differences in motivation of the two comparison groups.

The problem cited above can be avoided by having the researcher *assign* the subjects to the various treatment groups in a manner which insures that the subjects in the groups are approximately equal on all relevant characteristics. There are three general techniques for accomplishing this which will be discussed in this chapter. The first technique is called a *random-groups design* because subjects are randomly assigned to the separate treatments. The random assignment of subjects allows the experimenter to be fairly certain that the subjects in all treatments are approximately equal as to subject variables. The second technique is the *matched-groups design*. Using this design the experimenter first gets the scores for each subject on some task or test and then assigns subjects to the various treatment groups so that all of the treatment groups are equal with respect to these scores. The third technique is the *within-subject design*. Using this design all subjects participate in all experimental treatments which insures that the treatment groups are equal as to subject variables. In the first two techniques, random-groups design and matched-groups design, *different* subjects are assigned to the different experimental treatments. These two designs are called *independent-groups designs*. In the third technique, the within-subjects design, the same subjects participate in all experimental treatments.

RANDOM-GROUPS DESIGN

The most common method of assigning subjects to treatments is by a *random* assignment. In its most rigid form this would mean that a selection procedure is used so that each subject has an equal opportunity (or probability) of being assigned to each treatment group. If the experiment consisted of two treatment groups, one method of random assignment would be to flip a coin for each subject when he reports to the lab booth for the experimental session. If the coin lands on "heads" the subject is assigned to treatment A, and if it lands on "tails" the subject is assigned to treatment B. Using a randomization procedure such as this, the experimenter can be fairly certain that as a group the subjects in treatment A and subjects in treatment B are approximately equal.

While the above procedure is simple to administer and is consistent with the definition of random assignment, it also presents a serious problem. With this procedure it is quite possible that the experimenter will end up with unequal numbers of subjects in the two treatments. For example, it would be possible to end up with 15 subjects in treatment A and only five subjects in treatment B. This unequal number of subjects would be undesirable because the treatment mean based on the five would probably be less stable than a mean based on more subjects. A second consideration is that some of the statistical analyses of the results are simplified if equal numbers (n's) of subjects are used in each treatment group. Ideally, what is needed is a procedure that allows for some random assignment but also insures equal n's in each of the treatment groups. Such procedures are commonly used; and although they are not in accord with a rigid definition of random assignment, they are usually called "random assignment" or perhaps more accurately, "unbiased assignment."

In the Linder, Cooper, and Jones experiment (p. 24) in which the subjects were given $.50 or $2.50 for writing an essay, each subject reported to the lab booth individually and was assigned to a treatment when he appeared. Experiments of this type usually take place over periods of weeks or months, and an unbiased selection procedure must take into account the possibility that subjects who report earlier for the experiment may not have similar characteristics to those who report later for the experiment. For example, subjects who report later may have heard something about the experiment from subjects who report earlier, or perhaps the more motivated subjects appear earlier. One procedure to take this into account would be some form of "block randomization." Using this procedure the experiment is run in a series of "blocks" over the time period so that all treatments are represented within each block but the order in which they appear within the block is somewhat random. For example, in a two-treatment experiment the experimenter might flip a coin for the first subject who reports to the lab booth. If the coin lands "heads," the subject is assigned to treatment A, and if the coin lands "tails" the subject is assigned to treatment B. The next subject who reports to the lab booth is assigned to the treatment not assigned to the first subject. Thus if "heads" comes up for the first subject, he is assigned to treatment A and the second subject is assigned to treatment B. The coin is flipped for the third subject and the fourth subject is assigned the other treatment. This process is repeated until all 20 subjects have participated in the experiment. With this procedure the two treatments are equally distributed over the time period in which the experiment is conducted, but within each block there is unbiased assignment.

If more than two treatments are used in an experiment, block randomization can be used by putting slips of paper representing each treatment into a container and drawing one out as each subject reports for the experiment. For example, if six treatments are used, six slips of paper, each with a different letter representing the six different treatments, are put into a container. As each subject reports for the experiment one slip of paper is drawn out of the container, and the subject is assigned to the treatment represented by the letter on that slip. The slip is not put back into the container. The second subject is assigned to the treatment by drawing from the five remaining slips. This procedure is followed until all six slips have been drawn from the container. At this point all the slips are put back into the container and the procedure begins all over again.

The procedures covered in the preceding paragraphs are especially applicable to experiments in which subjects report to the experiment over an extended length of time. In another type of research, all subjects for the experiment are available to the experimenter at the same time. For example, in the Paul experiment (p. 11) comparing the effectiveness of insight and behavior therapy in treating speech phobia, the experimenter had the names of 67 students who exhibited speech phobia and had to assign them to the four experimental conditions. In the experiment on employment opportunity training (see p. 70), there were 60 applicants for the course offered by the center, and the director somehow had to assign half of these applicants to the treatment group and half to the control group. There are several ways of accomplishing an unbiased assignment for this type of problem and only a few of these will be discussed.

Suppose an experimenter has the names of 60 subjects and wants to assign 15 subjects to each of four treatment groups. One procedure would be to use the slips of paper and container method, except in this case 15 slips of paper with "A" marked on them would be placed in the container as well as 15 slips of paper with "B" marked on them, etc. The names of the subjects would be listed on a sheet in alphabetical order. As the experimenter went down the list, he would draw a slip of paper out of the container (but not replace the slip) for each name and assign that name to be in the treatment indicated by the letter on the slip. This same procedure might be simplified by arranging the names in random order (e.g., put each of the 60 names on a 3 × 5 index card and shuffle the cards in the same manner as you would playing cards) and then assign the first name on the list to treatment A, the second name to treatment B, . . . the fifth to treatment A, etc.

In some experiments the experimenter may not have the subjects' names before the experiment begins; however, all subjects report to the experiment at the same time. Suppose there are 60 subjects in a large room and these must be assigned to four treatments. Probably the simplest way would be to start at the front of the room and have the subjects count off by fours. All number 1's go into one treatment group, all number 2's into a second group, etc. This would seem to be an unbiased selection, assuming that the subjects are not seated in the room in some systematic manner. Frequently, subjects meet in a large room and the various treatments are represented in the materials in test booklets passed out to the subjects. For example, Johnson and Scileppi (1969) wanted to study change in attitude to plausible and implausible communications. These communications were in the form of written messages that appeared in different test booklets together with attitude scales to be filled out by the subjects. Groups of 10 to 20 subjects were tested at the same time in classrooms. The procedure used in this experiment was to shuffle the test booklets (as one would shuffle playing cards) before passing them out. In this way the experimenters were randomly assigning treatments to subjects rather than vice versa.

Even rather complex assignment problems can be handled fairly easily. For example, one of the writers conducted a group problem-solving experiment in which subjects met in groups of threes to solve a particular human relations problem. The independent variable was two types of instructions to the group which we shall call treatment A and treatment B. Thus the problem was not only to randomly assign three-person groups to treatments (A or B) but also to randomly assign subjects into three-person groups. To further complicate the assignment problem, one member of each three-person group was to be randomly assigned to be the leader of his group. Sixty subjects reported to a large classroom, and somehow the experimenter had to end up with 10 three-person groups in each of two treatments with a randomly assigned leader in each group. This assignment problem was easily solved by assigning each subject a number from 1 to 60 as he entered the room. The experimenter had a deck of 60 3 × 5 index cards, each with a number from 1 to 60 written on it. The experimenter shuffled the cards and then drew three cards off the top of the deck. The subject represented by the number on the first card drawn off the deck was designated as the leader of the group, and the subjects represented by the other two numbers were designated as members of the group. The experimenter kept drawing blocks of three cards off the top of the deck until all 20 groups were formed. The groups formed by the first 10 blocks of three cards were placed in treatment A, and the groups formed by the second 10 blocks of three cards were put into treatment B. Thus a rather complicated assignment process was handled very quickly and in a reasonably unbiased manner.

MATCHED-GROUPS DESIGN

Another way of insuring that all the treatment groups are equal as to subject characteristics is called matching. With the matching procedure all subjects are measured on some test or task that is assumed to be highly related to the task used in the actual experiment. The subjects then are assigned to the various treatment groups of the experiment on the basis of this pretest measure so that the treatment groups will be approximately equal with respect to pretest scores. With this assignment procedure the experimenter can be assured that all the treatment groups are equal with respect to one subject characteristic that is believed to be highly related to performance on the actual experimental task.

Before discussing matching techniques let us note the assumptions made when using this procedure. First, the researcher assumes that he knows what subject characteristic is highly related to performance on the experimental task, and secondly, he assumes that he can get scores for each subject on this characteristic. There is always a danger that the first assumption is invalid, and that the second condition cannot be met either because there is no good measure for the characteristic or because the experimenter cannot get the subjects' scores on that measure. Pretest tasks or tests may usually be divided into two major types. The first are tasks or tests that are quite different from the experimental task but are assumed to be highly related to the task. For example, it might be assumed that intelligence is highly related to a learning task and the experimenter would want to match on intelligence. In this case the pretest is an IQ test which is quite different from the actual experimental task. Another type of matching variable is a task that is quite similar (or identical) to the experimental task. Lambert and Solomon (1952) trained 20 rats to run down a runway at the end of which there was a goal box which contained food. After 30 acquisition trials the 20 rats were divided into two groups. One group of 10 rats was blocked (from going down the runway) at a point near the goal box (treatment A), and the other group of 10 rats was blocked near the beginning of the runway (treatment B). The dependent variable was the number of trials it took both groups of rats to extinguish their running response, and a rat was considered extinguished if it did not leave the start box within a three-minute time period. The researchers had recorded how long it took each rat to leave the start box on the last four acquisition trials. On the basis of these time scores they assigned (matched) the 20 rats to the two treatment groups so that, as a group. the two treatments were approximately equal as to time taken to leave the start box before the two treatments were initiated. In this example the matching was done on the same task as was used in the experimental session.

One technique for matching is through the use of *matched pairs*. With this technique the experimenter takes two subjects with identical scores on the matching variable and assigns one to treatment A and the second subject to treatment B. Suppose a two-treatment learning experiment is conducted and it is assumed that IQ is highly related to performance on the learning task.

First, IQ scores would be obtained for a large number of subjects. From this pool of subjects the experimenter would pick out two people with an IQ of 135 and put one in treatment A and one in treatment B. Then he would pick out two subjects with an IQ of 130 and put one in A and one in B. This process is repeated until he has the desired number of subjects in each treatment group. Here there is a perfect matching of subjects in the two treatments. The same procedure is used if there are more than two treatments, e.g., the experimenter would pick three subjects with IQ of 135 and assign one to each of the three treatment groups. Another example would be a drug therapy experiment on schizophrenics in which an experimenter might want to match on age. He would take two 50-year-old schizophrenics and put one in the drug therapy group and one in the placebo group. Next, he would take two 46-year-olds, . . . etc.

In the preceding paragraph *precise* matching of subjects was achieved. However, perhaps more frequently, this may not be possible. Suppose that in a rat experiment similar to that of Lambert and Solomon described above, the experimenter had eight rats and wanted to use a matched-pair technique to assign them to two treatments (A and B) based on the length of time it took them to leave the start box on the last acquisition trial. The times of the eight rats were 20.5, 17.2, 10.7, 8.0, 7.2, 6.5, 4.3, and 3.2 seconds. It is obvious that precise matching cannot be done since no two scores are alike. The experimenter is forced to use an ad lib matching procedure in which he attempts to balance out the scores. The following grouping of scores seems to be the best matching possible for the eight rats.

Treatment A	Treatment B
20.5	17.2
8.0	10.7
7.2	6.5
3.2	4.3
$\bar{x} = 9.72$	$\bar{x} = 9.67$

The means of both groups are approximately the same and both groups contain high, moderate, and low scoring rats.

Another matching technique that may be used is a random-blocks technique. Suppose that 80 schizophrenics were to be assigned to four treatment groups in a drug therapy experiment. The experimenter also wants to match them as to age since he has some evidence that the older the patient, the less favorably he responds to therapy. Using a random-block technique the experimenter would rank the ages of the 80 patients. He would then take the four oldest patients and *randomly* assign one to each of the four treatments, then he would take the four next oldest patients and randomly assign each of these to one of the four treatments, and so on until all 80 subjects have been assigned. Thus he is taking blocks of patients of approximately equal age and randomly assigning the patients within each block to a particular treatment.

Matching techniques can be very powerful techniques for eliminating any bias due to subject characteristics *if* the experimenter knows what subject variables are highly related to the experimental task and *if* he can get scores on these variables.

WITHIN-SUBJECT DESIGN

Another way of insuring that each treatment group is equal with regard to subject variables is to have all subjects participate in all treatments. Since the same subjects are participating in all treatments, it can be assumed that the treatment groups are equal as to subject variables. This type of design has been called a "subject as own control design" or a "within-subject design." The latter term seems preferable and derives its designation because comparisons between treatments are made within the same subject. This was used in the example-experiment exploring the relationship between the frequency of a tone and the absolute loudness threshold (p. 14). In this experiment each subject was tested at 10 levels of frequency (25, 50, etc.). The mean absolute threshold for the four subjects at each frequency level formed the points of the curve. It is in this type of an experiment that the within-subject design is most frequently used, i.e., experiments in which subjects are required to make numerous judgements to different stimuli (on different occasions), and these different stimuli can be considered the independent variable.

The within-subject design insures that subject characteristics are equal in all treatments, but the use of this design brings up an additional problem with regard to the *order* in which treatments or stimuli will be presented to the subject. The results might change rather dramatically because the subject's judgement of a particular stimulus may be influenced by his previous judgements. For example, it can be easily demonstrated that a subject's judgement of the lightness or heaviness of an object is in part determined by the heaviness of previously judged objects. In discrimination experiments the subject may become more accurate or proficient at a task as he makes more judgements. This is usually called a *practice effect*. The opposite phenomenon, a *fatigue effect*, can also occur if the subject becomes tired or bored and his proficiency decreases. To control for the effects of order of stimulus presentation, several designs are possible.

One method is the use of a *latin-square design*. Suppose 15 subjects are to judge three different stimuli (A, B, and C). Using a latin-square design, different orders of stimuli will be derived such that (a) each stimulus appears once within a single order, and (b) each stimulus appears once for each presentation. This is illustrated in the table below.

ORDER OF STIMULUS PRESENTATION

	POSITION 1	POSITION 2	POSITION 3
1. Five subjects	A	B	C
2. Five subjects	B	C	A
3. Five subjects	C	A	B

Five subjects receive the stimuli in the order A, B, C; five subjects receive a B, C, A order; and five subjects receive a C, A, B order. Note that stimulus A is judged or responded to once in position 1, once in position 2, and once in position 3. The same pattern is true for stimuli B and C. The means of the judgements of all 15 subjects to the three stimuli can then be compared. These means are independent of order effects because each stimulus appeared equally in each order position. Should the experimenter be interested in order effects, these can be examined by looking at the subjects' judgements of each stimulus as a function of the order position.

Another procedure for controlling for order effects is through the use of a random-blocks design similar to that described earlier in the chapter. Suppose that an experiment is conducted in which each subject is required to make 10 judgements on each of seven different stimuli. The seven stimuli are treated as a block and the order of presentation within the block is determined by some randomization procedure. The first block (of seven stimuli) is presented to the subject and after the subject responds to these the seven stimuli are randomized again and this new order constitutes the second block. This procedure is repeated eight more times to this subject until he has made 10 judgements on each of the seven stimuli. The same procedure is also repeated for each subject used in the experiment.

The within-subject design often appears very desirable because the same subjects are used in all treatments and therefore the researcher is sure that treatments are equal as to subject variables. It also appears desirable because fewer subjects could be used. However, the within-subject design cannot be used in many experiments simply because the treatments themselves negate this possibility. If an experiment was performed to compare rats reared in isolation with rats reared in groups, it is obvious that the same subjects could not be in both treatments. If an experiment is performed comparing high IQ subjects with low IQ subjects, or an experiment comparing one method of teaching French with a second method, it is apparent that independent groups of subjects have to be used in each treatment. For other experimental problems it may be much easier to use independent groups to test the hypothesis without going into any complicated procedure that may be needed for a within-subject design. The within-subject design seems to be most applicable to research problems, such as the experiment on the relationship between frequency and absolute threshold, in which subjects are required to make judgements on numerous different stimuli (on different occasions), and these stimuli can be considered the independent variable. Another type of an experiment that necessitates a within-subject design is one in which order effects are of major interest. If an experimenter is concerned with what happens when a subject switches from a high reward situation to a low reward situation (and vice versa), he would need the same subjects to participate in both conditions.

SUBJECT LOSS (ATTRITION)

We have discussed steps that are taken to insure that the subject characteristics in each treatment group are approximately equal. A related problem deals with subject *attrition* or the loss of subjects in the various treatment groups of an experiment. This problem occurs in experiments in which subjects have to participate in more than one session—subjects coming for the first session may not necessarily appear for the second session. Consider the following hypothetical example.

An "employment opportunities" center offered a four-week course designed to help unemployed young adults with the techniques and procedures for finding jobs. Classes were held each day and covered such topics as where to go for a job, what type of job to look for, how to fill out applications, and practice in taking psychological tests used for employee selection. Of the 60 young adults who signed up for the course, the director of the center randomly selected 30 to be in the course and used the other 30 as a control group to test the effectiveness of the course. The control group had no contact with the center and were simply told that there was no room in the course for them and that they would have to find a job on their own. The dependent variable was the percent of subjects in the two groups who had found jobs within a month after the course had ended. Of the 16 people (out of 30) who completed the course, 12 of them (75 percent) were employed within a month. Of the 30 control-group subjects, 15 of them (50 percent) were employed within this period. The director of the center took these results as evidence in support of his program noting that he had increased the number of employed by 25 percent.

Before criticizing this study, let us note that research of this type is difficult to do well; however, it is quite important research. Training programs such as these should be evaluated as to their effectiveness. There are many types of programs, e.g., therapy, counseling, remedial reading, leadership training, etc., that are very popular, but so far there is little research that examines their effectiveness.

The main concern in the above example is that the statistics are based only on the 16 subjects who completed the course out of

30 who started the course. The real question is who were the subjects who dropped out. They possibly were those who were less motivated about getting a job, or less intelligent and could not understand the materials in the course, or less emotionally stable and could not accept the routine of coming to the center every day. Thus the poor employment prospects may have been weeded out of the treatment group. On the other hand, it is difficult to drop out of a no-treatment control group, and all the poor employment prospects were still in that group. What the head of the center might have been doing is comparing a group of good employment prospects (the poor ones dropped out) versus a control group that consisted of both good and poor employment prospects. If this explanation is valid, then the effectiveness of the course is highly questionable.

In reality it is not known if the above explanation is valid; however, it seems to be a plausible explanation for the results. Any time there is a loss of subjects in an experiment, particularly if the loss is greater in one treatment group than another, it is important to find out the characteristics of those subjects who dropped out. One possibility would be to look at the employment rate of those who dropped out. If it is only about 25 percent, then it would seem to support the explanation that the poor employment prospects were weeded out. If it is around 50 percent (or higher), then the course would seem to be fairly effective.

The primary danger with subject attrition is that a select subgroup, e.g., low IQ subjects, may drop out of one treatment group but remain in another treatment group. If this occurs, then the treatment groups cannot be considered equal as to subject characteristics, and the results obtained may be due to subject differences rather than to treatment differences. It is important to have as much relevant information as possible on the subjects who dropped out in order to ascertain if they are some select subgroup. If this relevant information indicates that the dropouts are not a select subgroup but rather some "random" sample of the original treatment group, then the researcher may feel fairly confident that his results are not due to any particular subject differences. On the other hand, if this information indicates that the dropouts are some select subgroup, it may be possible to eliminate that subgroup in the other treatment groups and thus make the various treatment groups somewhat comparable.

Researchers can avoid problems of subject attrition by having subjects participate in only a single session. Thus there is no loss since there is no second session. If subjects are needed for more than one session, a standard procedure is to inform them before they start the experiment that they will be needed for more than one session and ask that they participate only if they can attend a second session. Frequently, a phone call will bring in those who have forgotten. In experiments in which subjects are needed for repeated testing for perhaps 10 days or so (as in some perception experiments), it is customary to pay the subjects and the subjects are hired only on the condition that they will complete the required number of sessions. In animal experiments attrition usually is not a problem since the subjects reside in your laboratory colony and can be used at will. However, there is always a danger in animal experiments of loss of subjects due to sickness or death, particularly if deprivation or stress treatments are used. For example, Bayoff (1940) compared the performance of rats reared in isolation versus rats reared in groups in a highly competitive stress situation. Ten of the isolation-reared rats died before the experiment was over; however, only one of the group-reared rats died.

Subject attrition problems should be avoided if possible by using one of the techniques stated in the preceding paragraph. If the study occurs over long periods of time, and attrition problems seem inevitable, it is important to get information on all subjects including the dropouts. Ideally, this information would include (a) pretreatment information, which might include intelligence data, motivation data, adjustment data, etc.; (b) data on the progress of the subjects up to the point at which they dropped out, e.g., learning or performance data; and (c) posttreatment data on all subjects such as employment rates in the above example. With this information the results of the experiment may be more easily interpreted.

DEFINITIONS

The following is a list of experimental design or procedure related concepts that were used in this chapter. Define each of the following:

field study

random-groups design

random assignment

block randomization

matched-groups design

within-subjects design

practice effect

fatigue effect

latin-square design

subject attrition

6

DESIGN CRITIQUES: II

The following are a series of experiment "briefs." There is a design problem in each of the briefs. You should critique and redesign each experiment in a manner similar to that done in Chapter 4. These briefs were chosen such that you need no expert technical knowledge of the research area being covered in the experiment.

EXPERIMENT BRIEFS

1.   A teacher of statistics wanted to compare two methods of teaching introductory statistics. One method relied heavily on the teaching of the theory behind statistics (Theory Method). The other method was labeled the Cookbook Method because it consisted of teaching the student various statistical tests and informing him as to when to use each test. This researcher found that a leading engineering school was using the Theory Method in all of its introductory statistics classes, and that a state teachers college was using the Cookbook Method in all of its classes. At the end of each semester he administered a standardized test on the applications of statistics to the statistics classes of both schools. The results of this testing indicated the classes that received the Theory Method were far superior to the classes that received the Cookbook Method. The researcher concluded that the Theory Method was the superior method and should be adopted by teachers of statistics.

2.   In an effort to determine the effects of the drug chlorpromazine on performance of schizophrenics, two clinical investigators randomly selected 20 acute schizophrenics from a mental hospital population. The task used was one in which several stimuli had to be put in order along a dimension, e.g., eight stimuli had to be ordered as to their weight. There were several tasks of this sort. The investigators used a within-subject design in which all subjects first performed the tasks after being injected with a saline solution (placebo) and then performed the tasks again (several hours later) after having been injected with chlorpromazine. Results indicated that fewer errors were made in the chlorproma-

zine treatment which suggested to the investigators that this drug facilitates more adequate cognitive functioning in this type of patient.

3. It was hypothesized that sensory deprivation inhibits the intellectual development of animals. To test this hypothesis an E used two rats, each of whom had just given birth to eight pups. One rat and her litter were placed in a large cage with ample space and with objects to explore. The pups of the second rat were separated from the mother and each was placed in a separate cage. These cages were quite small and the only objects they could see (or hear) were the four walls and the food dispenser. After five months, both treatment groups of rats were tested in a multiple-T maze using food as a reward. After 20 trials all of the nondeprived pups were running the maze without error. On the other hand, the deprived pups were still making several errors in the maze. This latter group of rats frequently "froze" in the start box and in the maze, and had to be prodded to move. The E concluded that sensory deprivation inhibits intellectual development such that deprived rats did not have the intellectual ability to learn even a simple maze.

4. During World War II an investigator attempted to examine the hypothesis that punishment is more effective for training people than reward. The problem he picked was the identification of enemy and of friendly airplanes. In his experimental situation, he had his subjects sit in front of what looked to be a radar screen. Silhouettes of enemy and of friendly airplanes were flashed on the screen in very short exposures (one second). As each silhouette was flashed on the screen, the subject had to respond by pressing one of two buttons — one button was marked "enemy," the other was marked "friendly." Each subject participated in the experiment for two hours on five successive days. On the first day, as each silhouette was flashed on the screen, the subject pressed one of the buttons and then was told by the E if he had been right or wrong in his identification. Starting on the second day, subjects were randomly assigned to one of two groups. The procedure was similar to the first day except in Group A the subjects were given 10 cents after every correct identification they made but were not punished for a wrong identification. In Group B, subject received an electric shock after every wrong identification they made but did not receive anything for a correct identification. This same procedure was continued for days three and four. The fifth day was considered the "test" day, and the subjects followed the same procedure except no reward, nor punishment, nor information from the E was given to the subject. The number of correct identifications for 100 silhouettes presented was considered a test of the effectiveness of each training method. As expected, there was some loss of subjects over the five-day period; about 5 percent of the Group A subjects and about 35

percent of the Group B subjects had dropped out of the experiment by the fifth day. Results indicated that on the 100 test trials given on the fifth day, the mean number of correct identifications for Group A was 80 and the mean for Group B was 92. The difference between the means was statistically significant. The E concluded that his hypothesis had been confirmed and suggested that all training programs be based on punishment.

5.   A YMCA official in a small town wanted some evidence to prove that his program was valuable in training future leaders. He went back to the membership records and got the names of those boys who were active members in his program 20 years ago. He also took school records and got the names of boys who were not YMCA members. He compared the two groups as to their occupations, salaries, etc., at the present and found that the YMCA group was doing much better. He concluded that this result was due to the influence of his program.

6.   A psychologist was interested in developing a test which would predict the success of prospective lawyers. He selected a random sample of lawyers listed in *Who's Who*, under the assumption that they would be "successful" lawyers. He then contacted them by means of a mail questionnaire which contained several hundred questions. The results were analyzed and a profile of successful lawyers was compiled. The questionnaire was given to a group of prospective law students, and those students whose scores were significantly divergent from the successful lawyer group were advised not to pursue a law career.

7.   A certain psychologist had a theory that as members of a group get to know each other better, the productivity of the group will increase up to a point and then will start to decrease slightly. The decrease ("the honeymoon is over" effect) is a point at which group members stop acting in a highly cooperative manner and start jostling for power, etc. To test this theory he formed groups of individuals who were strangers and had them work a series of tasks. There were five tasks, each taking 35 minutes to work, and he gave the groups a five-minute break between tasks. His results indicated that group productivity increased with the number of tasks up to the fifth task and for the fifth task there was a significant decrease in group performance. On the basis of the evidence he considered his theory supported.

8.   A clinical researcher examined whether interviews with patients or objective tests are better in the diagnosis of the patient's problems and outcomes. The experiment took place at a large mental hospital. In one group, 10 clinical psychology students each interviewed six new patients (during their internship at the hospital). The length of each interview was

one to two hours long. Another group of 60 patients were given a battery of standardized psychological tests (e.g., the MMPI) and the test results were interpreted by three clinical psychologists who had several years of experience in interpreting tests for the hospital. Each psychologist interpreted the test results for 20 patients. Both groups were asked to list the patient's major problems and to assign the patient to a diagnostic category (e.g., process schizophrenic, reactive schizophrenic, etc.). They were also asked to predict how long the patient would be in the hospital before he would improve to the extent that he could be released. Results indicate that the interviewers were 67 percent accurate in predicting diagnostic categories and 22 percent accurate in predicting length of stay. The "test" group was about 83 percent accurate in predicting diagnostic categories and 65 percent accurate in predicting length of stay. The experimenter concluded that interviews are of questionable value in either diagnosis or prediction of outcome and should be discontinued.

9.   An E wanted to test the hypothesis that males are more creative than females. He also hypothesized that the male superiority in creativity would be heightened under ego-involving conditions. The design used was a 2 × 2 factorial design in which one variable was sex and the other variable was high and low ego-involvement. He manipulated ego-involvement by telling half of the Ss that this task was a measure of how intelligent they are and that he would post their scores on a bulletin board (high ego-involvement). He told the other half of the Ss that he was developing the task and wanted to check its reliability and further told them not to put their names on the answer sheets (low ego-involvement). His test of creativity was an "Unusual Uses" test in which a person is given the name of an object (e.g., hammer) and he has to write down as many different unusual uses for that object as he can in five minutes. Twenty-five males and 25 females participated in each of the two ego-involvement conditions. The males were members of a senior ROTC class and the females were obtained from sorority pledge classes. Two objects were used: (1) army compass, and (2) monkey wrench. Ss were given five minutes for each object. The results indicated that the mean number of unusual uses for the two objects for males was 4.1 under low ego-involvement and 7.6 under high ego-involvement. The means for the females were 3.2 under low ego-involvement and 2.4 under high ego-involvement. Since both the main effects and the interaction effect were statistically significant using analysis of variance, the E concluded that his hypotheses were supported.

ANALYSIS OF EXPERIMENTS

In this part, several research articles are reviewed. These articles were selected to represent a variety of topics and design procedures. Having carried out an experiment, the psychologist's next obligation is to report its results to the scientific community. In practice this means preparing a research paper for a journal read by other psychologists. The ability to write such papers and to read them with understanding is therefore one of the most important demands upon the professional psychologist.

Because journal space is limited and because there are so many other demands on the time of the scientist, a premium is placed on clarity and conciseness in the presentation of research results. At the same time, because the articles are aimed at other scientists, particularly those working in the same problem area, a knowledge of that area's research history and its methodologies is taken for granted, which makes journal articles difficult going not only for students but sometimes for psychologists with different research specialties.

The articles are presented as they appeared in the psychological journals. Each article is followed by an analysis which attempts to explain exactly why the researcher did what he did. By repeated exposure to and careful analysis of such papers, the student may come to feel comfortable in reading research reports and he may develop an understanding of principles of experimental design in psychology.

A highly stylized format is used for the reporting of experimental results and usually follows the guidelines stated in the Publication Manual of the American Psychological Association (1967). The format is very similar from journal to journal and contains the sections which are described below.

1.   *Title*. The title should be a clear, brief statement of the subject under inquiry. Authors frequently suggest a statement of "the effects of . . . on . . ." which gives the reader a clue as to the independent and dependent variables. The title is followed by the author's name and affiliation.

2.   *Review of Literature*. Articles typically begin with a brief historical review of major issues and previous results in the area. The results of other researchers are presented in a logical sequence so that the current experiment fits into a series of experimental developments.

3.   *Problem and Hypothesis*. The statement of the problem identifies the issues to be dealt with. The statement of the problem and the statement of the hypothesis are frequently contained in a single paragraph, if not in a single sentence. The statement of the hypothesis may follow an "if . . . then . . ." clause. Frequently the independent and dependent variables are identified in this section.

4.   *Method*. This section explains the experimental design in sufficient detail to allow replication of the study. There are usually three parts: (1) subjects (*S*s), (2) apparatus or materials, and (3) procedure. All independent variables and other variables which may affect the results are identified and, if necessary, controlled. If a procedure has been previously described by an earlier researcher, then it is permissible to simply cite the original source.

5.   *Results*. In this section, the data generated by the experiment and the analysis of that data are reported. In addition to its presentation in the text, the data may be presented in tabular or graphic form. Because of space limitations, an attempt is made to present as much pertinent material as possible in the most succinct form. All graphs and tables must have some explanation within the text. It is impractical to present the data for every subject. Therefore, in summarizing his results the experimenter should employ those statistical techniques which most clearly convey his findings.

6.   *Discussion*. The purpose of this section is to interpret the results of the experiment, i.e., to point out any reservations about the results; to note similarities or differences between these results and the findings of other investigators; to suggest future research; and especially to note the implications of the results to theory and/or practice in the specific research area.

7.   *Summary*. This section may appear at the end or beginning of the article and it contains a brief description of the procedure and results.

8.   *References*. All material cited in the article should be noted in this section. The general format is: author(s) name(s), title, journal, publication year, volume, and pages.

The use of the above format allows the reader to progress in a logical manner. As you read and review a variety of articles, you will find this style to be an expeditious means to present information. There is no "right" way to read an article, but listed below are some suggestions as to how you might try to understand research reports.

First, read the title and try to establish the general category within psychology that the study is investigating. For example, "Two-phase model for human classical conditioning" (Prokasy & Harsanyi, *Journal of Experimental Psychology*, 1968, *78*, 359–368). You probably have had some experience with "classical conditioning" and know something of the famous Pavlovian studies with dogs. These authors have apparently studied learning by using a conditioning method and have developed some model to describe their results. In addition to simply reading a title, it is suggested that you try to raise concrete questions about the problem and procedures. In the case of the example, you might ask "How did the authors condition a human—with a bell and meat powder?" "What are two possible phases to classical conditioning?"

Most journal articles contain an abstract at the beginning or end of the paper. The major findings and method used are briefly described. A careful reading of this, coupled with an inquiring mind, will facilitate your understanding of the paper.

A quick scan of the entire paper, with greater emphasis on the review of literature, hypothesis, and discussion than on specific details of the methods and results sections is suggested. Scanning the paper and the preceding two steps will allow you to get a general impression of the author's intent. You may want to return to the abstract to reestablish a point of view, but the critical aspect of scientific reading is a probing inquiry. As you review and read, *question*!

Finally, read the article in its entirety, sorting out data from discussion. During the reading, you should examine how the author controlled for variables, and how he specifically treated the data.

In reading an article, you might ask yourself some of these questions, plus many more which would be determined, in part, by the responses to questions.

1. What is this research all about?
2. What is the general problem?

3. What are the results of others?
4. What is the hypothesis?
5. What type of materials did the author use?
6. How does he operationally define his variables?
7. What controls does he use?
8. How does he analyze his data?
9. How does he interpret his data?
10. Who does he cite as relevant investigators in the area?
11. Can I improve on this study?
12. What additional work needs to be done?
13. Can the data be interpreted in another way?

Some articles are so complex or use so much jargon that you may have difficulty in understanding them. This experience is not uncommon among new students (as well as some old students). Repeat the process of reading and questioning suggested above. Sometimes students find it helpful to review an article for a friend and allow him to ask questions.

7

IDENTIFICATION OF COLAS

IDENTIFICATION OF COLA BEVERAGES
Frederick J. Thumin, *Washington University*

An attempt was made to overcome certain methodological inadequacies of earlier studies in determining whether cola beverages can be identified on the basis of taste. Some 79 Ss completed questionnaires on their cola drinking habits and brand preferences, then were tested individually on samples of cola beverages presented under methods of paired comparisons. Significant chi square values were obtained for Coca Cola and Pepsi Cola, due to the large number of correct identifications for these brands. Correct identification of Royal Crown, however, did not differ from chance expectancy. No significant relationship was found between ability to identify cola beverages and degree of cola consumption; nor were Ss any better at identifying their "regular" brand than they were other brands.[1]

Earlier studies attempting to determine whether cola beverages can be identified on the basis of taste[2] have, in the main, obtained negative results (Bowles & Pronko, 1948; Pronko & Bowles, 1948; Pronko & Bowles, 1949; Pronko & Herman, 1950; Prothro, 1953). These results may, in part, be attributed to certain methodological difficulties. For example, in the

Reprinted by permission from *Journal of Applied Psychology*, 1962, *46* (5), 358–360. Published by the American Psychological Association.

[1] The author wishes to express his appreciation to A. Barclay who served as critical reader for earlier drafts of this paper.

[2] In this report, the word "taste" is used in the broad sense; i.e., to include gustation, olfaction, and possible tactual qualities as well.

majority of these studies, the subjects were not informed as to

a what brands they were attempting to identify. This lack of restriction encouraged guessing behavior, which resulted in the naming of irrelevant beverages (e.g., Dr. Pepper), as well as relatively frequent mentions of the more heavily advertised brands such as Coca Cola.

Moreover, the subjects were expected to identify the various colas on the basis of past experience, yet apparently no attempt was made to determine whether the subjects had ever tasted

b these beverages, or to relate identification to degree of cola consumption.

Each of these previous studies used essentially the same method of stimulus presentation; namely, all beverages were

c presented simultaneously to the subject, and only one such presentation was made. This technique, while satisfactory, would appear to be somewhat less sensitive than the method of paired comparisons, which requires the subject to identify each brand a number of times under various experimental conditions.

Thus, the purpose of the present study was to determine whether methodological inadequacies in the earlier studies may have contributed to the subjects' relative inability to identify brands. The primary modifications in experimental design were as follows: an indication of cola consumption habits was

d obtained, subjects were told in advance what beverages they were attempting to identify, and the method of paired comparisons was used for presentation of stimuli.

METHOD

Seventy-nine subjects were employed, all of whom were either college students or college graduates between the ages of 18 and 37 years. The subjects were first asked to fill out a questionnaire on their cola consumption habits and brand preferences. The cola beverages were presented to the subjects individually in an experi-

e mental room which was kept dimly lighted to eliminate possible visual cues. Instructions were as follows:

I would like to have you taste and identify some cola drinks. I will place two cups at a time in front of you—one on your left and one on your right. Taste these two colas in any order you wish; then tell me what brand you think each one is. Be careful not to change the position of the cups while you are tasting them; that is, keep the left cup on the left, and the right cup on the right. Each time you finish with one pair of cups, rinse your mouth well by taking a few swallows of water from the water cup. When you have done this, I will give you the next pair.

There are three colas involved in this study—Cola Cola, Pepsi Cola, and Royal Crown. Even if you are not sure of the brand in some cases, I still want you to tell me what brand you *think* it is. The two members of a pair are always different brands; that is, a brand is never compared with itself. Are there any questions?

Using the method of paired comparisons, six pairs of beverages were presented to the subject, one pair at a time. The subjects were exposed to each brand four times for a total of 12 judgements. The order of presentation of stimulus pairs was randomly determined. Stimulus cups contained 2 ounces of the beverage at an approximate temperature of 5° centigrade.

RESULTS

f   The chi square was used to determine whether ability to identify brands differed significantly from chance expectancy. As Table 1 shows, the chi square values for both Coca Cola

g   and Pepsi Cola were significant at the .01 level of confidence, while that for Royal Crown was not significant. Inspection of the data indicates that the significant divergencies obtained with Coca Cola and Pepsi Cola are due to the large number of correct identifications of these brands; for example, more than twice the expected number of subjects were able to identify these brands correctly at least three times out of four.

The results presented in Table 2 indicate that ability to identify cola beverages correctly was unrelated to degree of consumption; i.e., correct identifications were essentially the same for heavy, medium, and light cola drinkers. Further analysis of the data showed that ability to identify a given brand was also unrelated to whether that brand was considered by the subject to be his "regular" brand.

Table 1 Chi Square for Observed and Expected Frequencies of Brand Identification

BRAND OF COLA	OBSERVED AND EXPECTED FREQUENCIES	NUMBER OF CORRECT IDENTIFICATIONS				
		0	1	2	3 or 4	x^2
Coca Cola	(f_0)	13	23	24	19	14.57**
Pepsi Cola	(f_0)	12	20	26	21	22.14**
Royal Crown	(f_0)	18	28	19	14	4.60*
All brands	$(f_e)^a$	15.6	31.2	23.4	8.8	

Note. For each comparison, $df = 3$.
^{a}Expected values were obtained from the expression $N(1/3p + 2/3q)^4$. Each sample had one chance in three of being identified correctly, and each brand was presented to the subject four times.
*$p > .05$.
**$p < .01$.

By telling the subjects in advance what brands they were attempting to identify, irrelevant brand naming was eliminated as well as excessive naming of heavily advertised brands. Specifically, Coca Cola was mentioned 317 times, Pepsi Cola 321 times, and Royal Crown 310 times.

Table 2 Chi Square for Brand Identification as Related to Consumption

NUMBER OF COLAS CONSUMED PER WEEK	NUMBER OF CORRECT IDENTIFICATIONS		
	0–3	4–6	7–12
Heavy	10	14	3
(7 or more)	(8.5)	(12.0)	(6.5)
Medium	7	9	10
(3–6)	(8.2)	(11.5)	(6.3)
Light	8	12	6
(0–2)	(8.2)	(11.5)	(6.3)

Note. Expected values appear in parentheses.
$x^2 = 5.44$, $df = 4$; $p > .05$.

DISCUSSION

h The present study clearly demonstrated that certain brands of cola can be identified on the basis of taste. The significant chi square values obtained with Coca Cola and Pepsi Cola were due to the large number of correct identifications for these brands. The subjects' inability to identify Royal Crown Cola can probably be attributed to a lack of *recent* exper-

i ience with this brand. Some 58 percent of the subjects said they had not had a Royal Crown for at least 6 months prior to the experiment.

No relationship was found between ability to identify cola beverages and degree of cola consumption (i.e., number of colas consumed in an average week). Moreover, the subjects were no better at identifying their regular brand than they were at identifying other brands. Thus, it would appear that the the subjects needed a certain minimal amount of recent experience with a brand in order to identify it, but beyond this minimal amount, additional experience (i.e., heavier consumption) did not help.

j Within the framework of this study, the method of paired comparisons proved to be sufficiently sensitive to detect small but significant abilities to identify cola beverages. There appeared to be no problem with the development of sensory adaptation as successive pairs of stimuli were presented. Analysis of the data revealed that, as trials progressed, the subjects showed small (though nonsignificant) increases in ability to identify brands.

REFERENCES

Bowles, J. W., Jr., & Pronko, N. H. Identification of cola beverages: II. A further study. *J. appl. Psychol.*, 1948, *32*, 559–564.

Pronko, N. H., & Bowles, J. W., Jr. Identification of cola beverages: I. First study. *J. appl. Psychol.*, 1948, *32*, 304–312.

Pronko, N. H., & Bowles, J. W., Jr. Identification of cola beverages: III. A final study. *J. appl. Psychol.*, 1949, *33*, 605–608.

Pronko, N. H., & Herman, D. T. Identification of cola beverages: IV. Postscript. *J. appl. Psychol.*, 1950, *34*, 68–69.

Prothro, E. T. Identification of cola beverages overseas. *J. appl. Psychol.*, 1953, *37*, 494–495.

CASE ANALYSIS

Most of us have debated the distinguishability of certain consumer products. For example, the devotee of a certain brand of soft drink may characterize his choice by some distinct quality of the drink. The author of this research is asking the question "How identifiable are cola beverages when tasted under controlled conditions?" This is an experiment in applied psychology since there is no attempt to test or develop any theory of behavior. Rather the experimenter has taken three consumer products and tested to determine if people can distinguish between the three.

This experiment has several distinguishing features which you should examine. One of these features is the use of the method of paired comparison. This technique is used when the items to be judged cannot be easily measured by some independent scale. If a similar experiment were conducted by a chemist, he may use a variety of scales to identify different colas (e.g., effervescence, color, chemical composition, etc.). The psychologist's task is more difficult in the respect that he must resort to a subjective evaluation. Thumin has used an empirically sound method (paired comparison) to evaluate a subjective judgement.

REVIEW OF LITERATURE, STATEMENT OF PROBLEM, AND HYPOTHESIS

The first paragraph attempts to briefly describe the previous research on cola identification and to note the scope of the present research. Although it is not common to define terms in research papers, the author uses an acceptable method to define "taste" in a footnote.

Three methodological factors (**a**, **b**, and **c**) were not well controlled in the previous literature which may have an effect on cola identification. They are (**a**) not informing the subjects of the colas to be identified, (**b**) no control over subjects' experience with cola beverages, and (**c**) subjects received all colas simultaneously. Following each of these possible contaminating factors, the author tentatively identifies the possible biasing (or confounding) result of these uncontrolled factors.

In (d) a succinct statement of the methodological differences between this and previous studies is made.

The method of paired comparison was used, which is a standard technique in which a subject is given two stimuli and asked to judge them. The judgement in the present study was a qualitative one, i.e., subjects were asked to identify specific colas by taste. (It should be noted that the method of comparison also permits quantitative judgements. Under these circumstances, the subjects would be asked to identify greater or lesser amounts of a certain quality.) A related procedure, and one mentioned by Thumin in (c) as the predominant procedure used in cola tasting, is called multiple comparison. In this method, subjects are asked to make judgements on a variety of stimuli.

This study does not clearly state an hypothesis to be tested, yet the reader can provide his own statement of an hypothesis with the material presented. How would you state the hypothesis?

METHOD

The method section of this report is fairly brief but it contains the necessary information (including the exact instructions given to the subjects) to allow the study to be replicated. However, there are some features of the design that the author does not make explicit which we shall discuss here.

Type of Design

This design is quite similar to the design used for investigating the relationship between the frequency of a tone and the subject's sensitivity to that tone (p. 14) and is typical of the type of design found in these areas. In the present experiment the independent variable is three types of colas, whereas in the audition experiment the independent variable was tones of different frequencies. In the audition experiment the dependent variable was the absolute threshold of the tone, i.e., some hypothetical point above which the subject can hear the tone and below which he cannot hear the tone. In the present experiment the dependent variable is the correctness of the identification of the cola, i.e., can he or can he not correctly identify it. In both experiments there were multiple presentations of the same stimulus, e.g., in the audition experiment there were six attempts at threshold determination for each tone, three using the descending method and three using the ascending method. In the cola experiment the subjects were exposed to each brand four times. By using several presentations of the same stimulus, the experimenter may get a more stable or reliable measure of each subject's judgements. The basic difference in the two experiments is that in the audition experiment the experimenter only presented one tone at a time. This was an appropriate method for that problem because the experimenter was asking "When can you hear the tone?" In the Thumin experiment, the problem is identifying the cola, i.e. "Which cola is it?" To get an answer to this question Thumin has argued that presenting two stimuli at the same time (paired-comparison method) is a more sensitive method than the other methods previously used.

Control Problems

It has previously been suggested (p. 39) that there are two types of control. The first is when the experimenter makes something occur and the second type is when he prevents something from occurring (extraneous variables). We have discussed the first type; let us now look at the extraneous variables that were controlled for.

Relations Between Pairs.   One cola may be easy to identify when presented with a second cola but difficult to distinguish from a third. For example, Coke may be easier to correctly identify when it is paired with Royal Crown but difficult to identify when it is paired with Pepsi. To avoid problems such as this each cola was paired with each other cola an equal number of times. Another problem is that within each pair presentation the first cola may be easier to identify than the second cola or vice versa. To eliminate this problem each cola could have been presented first and second in the pair an equal number of times. While Thumin did not systematically control for this, it could easily have been incorporated into the design to strengthen the procedure.

Order Effects.   It has previously been pointed out (p. 67) that when subjects make a series of judgements, order effects can appear. The subject may become more sensitive with practice or he may become fatigued and his judgements become poorer. In taste experiments it is very probable that his judgements may become poorer since not all of the cola may be washed out of his mouth on each trial and the residue may confuse later judgements. To control for this Thumin presented the stimulus pairs in random order. This procedure is described in Chapter 5 (p. 68) and is an effective method for controlling order effects.

Stimulus Accumulation.   Related to the preceding point, the subject washed out his mouth with water after each pair was judged. This control procedure attempts to eliminate the confusion of taste from one pair to the next. It is reasonable to assume that the subject could not have very sensitive judgement for a given pair if the taste of the previous pair was still in his mouth. Further, clean cups are used for each presentation to eliminate the possibility of an accumulation of cola in the cups.

Visual Cues.   Thumin was testing to see whether or not the subjects could identify the colas by taste. To do this he had to eliminate any other cues that might help the subject identify the cola. One such set of cues are visual cues, e.g., Coke may look different from Pepsi. To eliminate the visual cues, the experiment took place in a dimly lighted room. Frequently, experimenters will blindfold subjects in experiments of this type to eliminate any possibility of visual cues.

Temperature.   Most people drink colas that are cooled to a temperature of 5° Centigrade (46° Fahrenheit). Their experience with tasting cola is limited to this temperature, i.e., the taste of Coke is really the taste of Coke at 5° C. To allow for this, Thumin presented all colas at a constant temperature of 5° C.

Guessing.   In many judgement experiments, a problem arises with respect to the subjects' guessing at the identification. Some subjects will guess when they do not know the correct identification and some subjects will simply say that they do not know. To avoid these problems Thumin had all subjects guess at the correct identification when they did not know. He is quite explicit about this in his instructions when he points out to the subjects that even if they are not sure of the brand they should tell him what brand they *think* it is.

Note also that Thumin has (in a sense) corrected for guessing in his statistical analysis (see footnote to Table 1). There are three choices: one choice is correct and two are incorrect. Thus the probability of being correct is one out of three. The statistic is testing to see if the subjects' identifications were more correct than would be expected by chance.

Subject Variables.   Chapter 5 presented a lengthy discussion of the problem of subject variables in research. Much of this discussion centered around the problem of having people in one experimental treatment who are different as to some subject characteristics than are people in another treatment. Thumin has avoided this problem by having all subjects participate in all treatments, a *within-subject design.* It has also been pointed out above that Thumin has controlled for some of the problems of the within-subject design by controlling for order effects. However, another subject variable problem could appear in this experiment. Suppose that only those subjects who are heavy cola drinkers are those who can distinguish between the different brands. Let us further suppose that the sample of subjects Thumin picked had a small proportion of heavy cola drinkers. Because the sample contains only a few heavy drinkers (who can make correct identifications) and a high proportion of light drinkers (who cannot make correct identifications), then the majority of light drinkers might make it appear as if the identification of cola beverages is little better than chance. Thumin protected himself from this subject variable problem by finding out how much cola each subject drank per week. It is apparent that this subject variable did not influence the data (see Table 2); however, Thumin took into account this possibility and did test to see what effect this subject variable had on the dependent variable.

The above discussion of design and control procedures should make it evident to the student that careful planning is needed before an experiment is executed. It was pointed out in Chapter 3 that control problems vary with each experimental area. The Thumin experiment illustrates some of the considerations that must be taken into account in experimenting with the identification of the taste of substances.

RESULTS

The basic findings and a summary of the statistical analysis is the principle part of this section.

The χ^2 (pronounced "chi square") statistical procedure was used to treat the data (**f**). This is a relatively simple procedure in which the obtained results are compared with the results one would expect by chance alone. The logic is that if the obtained results vary greatly from the results expected by chance, then probably some experimental conditions are responsible for this diversity.

The level of confidence (**g**) is a reflection of the probability that the results would be obtained by chance alone. In the present study, the author establishes a level of confidence or $p = .01$, that is, the probability that such results would be obtained by chance alone is one in 100. Frequently, the level of confidence is set at .05 (or 5 in 100), and in some research it may be useful to demand even lower levels.

The author makes a clear summary statement of the identifiability of colas and also provides the reader with two tables which contain the data obtained. It is noted that the obtained χ^2 values exceed the .01 level and are actually significant beyond the .005 level.

DISCUSSION

In this section the author reviews the major findings (**h**) and offers a plausible explanation for the nonsignificant findings regarding the Royal Crown condition (**i**).

Finally, the sensitivity of using a paired-comparison technique is mentioned (**j**).

QUESTIONS

1.   In the design of this experiment (a) each cola was paired with each other cola an equal number of times, and (b) the presentation of stimulus pairs was randomly determined. From the theory presented concerning within-subject designs (Chapter 5), lay out exactly how one sequence of 12 pairs might have been presented to a subject.

2.   Why was a dimly lighted room used? (**e**) What effects would a red illuminated room have? A green illuminated room? A nonilluminated room? Would these conditions be worthy of research?

3.   Why did the subjects rinse their mouths? Should they eat something neutral (e.g., a cracker) between tests? Do you think this is a critical variable?

4.   What interpretation would you give to the fact that some subjects could not correctly identify the beverages? What factors may determine their preference for one cola over another? Would they be a more suggestible group?

5.   No sex differences were noted in the selection of subjects. Why? Subjects were not asked to identify their favorite cola. What influence might this have on the results?

6.   Design an experiment to test whether or not subjects can correctly identify whole, skim, and powdered milk.

7.   Design an experiment to test whether whole, skim, or powdered milk tastes better.

8

THE CREATIVE PORPOISE

THE CREATIVE PORPOISE: TRAINING FOR NOVEL BEHAVIOR

Karen W. Pryor, *Oceanic Institute*
Richard Haag, *Makapuu Oceanic Center*
Joseph O'Reilly, *University of Hawaii*

Two rough-toothed porpoises (*Steno bredanensis*) were individually trained to emit novel responses, which were not developed by shaping and which were not previously known to occur in the species, by reinforcing a different response to the same set of stimuli in each of a series of training sessions. A technique was developed for transcribing a complex series of behaviors on to a single cumulative record so that the training sessions of the second animal could be fully recorded. Cumulative records are presented for a session in which the criterion that only novel behaviors would be reinforced was abruptly met with four new types of responses, and for typical preceding and subsequent sessions. Some analogous techniques in the training of pigeons, horses, and humans are discussed.[1]

a The shaping of novel behavior, that is, behavior that does not occur or perhaps cannot occur, in an animal's normal activity, has been a preoccupation of animal trainers for centuries. The fox-terrier turning back somersaults, the elephant balancing on one front foot, or ping-pong playing pigeons (Skinner, 1962) are produced by techniques of successive approximation, or shaping. However, novel or original be-

Reprinted by permission from *Journal of the Experimental Analysis of Behavior*, 1969, *12*, 653–661. Copyright 1969 by the Society for the Experimental Analysis of Behavior, Inc.

a havior that is not apparently produced by shaping or differential reinforcement is occasionally seen in animals. Originality is a fundamental aspect of behavior but one that is rather difficult to induce in the laboratory.

In the fall of 1965, at Sea Life Park at the Makapuu Oceanic Center in Hawaii, the senior author introduced into the five daily public performances at the Ocean Science Theater a demonstration of reinforcement of previously unconditioned behavior. The subject animal was a female rough-toothed porpoise, *Steno bredanensis*, named Malia.

Since behavior that had been reinforced previously could no longer be used to demonstrate this first step in conditioning, it was necessary to select a new behavior for reinforcement in each demonstration session. Within a few days, Malia began emitting an unprecedented range of behaviors, including aerial flips, gliding with the tail out of the water, and "skidding" on the tank floor, some of which were as complex as responses normally produced by shaping techniques, and many of which were quite unlike anything seen in Malia or any other porpoise by Sea Life Park staff. It appeared that the trainer's criterion, "only those actions will be reinforced which have not been reinforced previously", was met by Malia with the presentation of complete patterns of gross body movement in which novelty was an intrinsic factor. Furthermore,

[1] Contribution No. 35, the Oceanic Institute, Makapuu Oceanic Center, Waimanalo, Hawaii. Carried out under Naval Ordinance Testing Station Contract # N60530-12292, NOTS, China Lake, California. A detailed account of this experiment, including the cumulative records for each session, has been published as NOTS Technical Publication # 4270 and may be obtained from the Clearing House for Federal Scientific and Technical Information, U.S. Department of Commerce, Washington, D.C. A 16-mm film, "Dolphin Learning Studies", based on this experiment, has been prepared by the U.S. Navy. Persons wishing to view this film may inquire of the Motion Picture Production Branch, Naval Undersea Warfare Center, 201 Rosecrans Street, San Diego, California 92132. The authors wish to thank Gregory Bateson of the Oceanic Institute, Dr. William Weist of Reed College, Oregon, and Dr. Leonard Diamond of the University of Hawaii for their extensive and valuable assistance; also Dr. William McLean, Technical Director, Naval Undersea Research and Development Center, San Diego, California, for his interest and support. Reprints may be obtained from Karen W. Pryor, Sea Life, Inc., Makapuu Oceanic Center, Waimanalo, Hawaii 96795.

the trainers could not imagine shaped behaviors as unusual as some emitted spontaneously by the porpoise.

b To see if the training situation used with Malia could again produce a "creative" animal, the authors repeated Malia's training, as far as possible, with another animal, one that was not being used for public demonstrations or any other work at the time. A technique of record keeping was developed to **c** pin-point if possible the events leading up to repeated emissions of novel behaviors.

METHOD

d A porpoise named Hou, of the same species and sex as Malia, was chosen. Hou had been trained to wear harness and instruments and to participate in physiological experiments in the open sea (Norris, 1965). This individual had a large repertoire of shaped responses but its "spontaneous activity" had never been reinforced. Hou was considered by Sea Life Park trainers to be "a docile, timid individual with little initiative."

e Training sessions were arranged to simulate as nearly as possible Malia's five brief daily sessions. Two to four sessions were held daily, lasting from 5 to 20 min each, with rest periods of about half an hour between sessions. Hou was given normal rations; it is not generally necessary to reduce food intake or body weight in cetaceans to make food effective as a reinforcer. Any food not earned in training sessions was given freely to the animal at the end of the day, and it was fed normal rations, without being required to work, on weekends. During the experimental period, no work was required of Hou other than that in the experiment itself. A bell was rung at the beginning and end of sessions to serve as a context marker. The appearance and positioning of the trainers served as an additional stimulus that the opportunity for reinforcement was now present.

f To record the events of each session, the trainer and two observers, one above water and one watching the underwater area through the glass tank walls, wore microphones and made a verbal commentary; earphones allowed the experimenters to hear each other. The three commentaries, and the sound of the conditioned reinforcer, the whistle, were recorded on a single tape. A typed transcript was made of each tape; then, by comparing transcript to tape, the transcript was marked at 15-sec intervals. Each response of the animal was then graphed on a cumulative record, with a separate curve to indicate each type of response in a given session (Fig. 2 to 6). It was necessary to make a relatively arbitrary decision about what constituted, a reinforceable or recordable act. In general, a rein-forceable act consisted of <u>any movement that was not part of the</u> <u>normal swimming action of the animal, and which was sufficiently</u> **g** <u>extended through space and time to be reported by two or more</u> <u>observers.</u> Such behavior as eye-rolling, inaudible whistling, and gradual changes in direction may have occurred, but they could not be distinguished by the trainers and therefore could not be reinforced, except coincidentally. This unavoidable contingency probably had the effect of increasing the incidence of gross motor responses. Posi-tion and sequence of responses were not considered. An additional criterion, which had been a contingency in much of Hou's previous training, was that only one type of response would be reinforced per session.

The experimental plan of reinforcing a new type of response in each session was not fully met. Sometimes a previously reinforced response was again chosen for reinforcement, to strengthen the response, to increase the general level of responding, or to film a given behavior. Whether the "reviewing" of responses was helpful or detrimental to the animal's progress is open to speculation.

Inter-observer reliability was judged from the transcripts of the taped sessions, in which a new behavior was generally recognized in concert by the observers. Furthermore, each new behavior chosen for reinforcement was later diagrammed in a series of position **h** sketches. At no time did any of the three observers fail to agree that the drawings represented the behaviors witnessed. These behavior diagrams were matched, at the end of the experiment, with film of each behavior, and were found to represent adequately the topog-raphy of those behaviors that had been reinforced (see Fig. 1).

After 32 training sessions, the topography of Hou's aerial be-haviors became so complex that, while undoubtedly novel, the behaviors exceeded the powers of the observers to discriminate and describe them. This breakdown in observer reliability was one factor in the termination of the experiment.

Steno bredanensis, the species of which Hou and Malia are members, has not been kept in captivity in the United States except at Sea Life Park. Therefore, data pertaining to normal behavior, plentiful for more common species such as *Tursiops truncatus*, are lacking. To corroborate the experimenters' observation that certain of Hou's responses were not in the normal repertoire of the species, and constituted genuine novelties, the diagrams of each reinforced behavior were shown or sent to the 12 past and present staff members who had had occasion to work with animals of this species. Each trainer was asked to rank the 16 behaviors in order of frequency of occurrence in a free-swimming untrained animal.

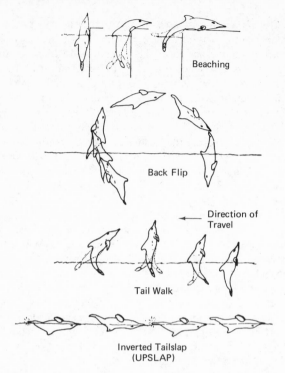

Beaching

Back Flip

Direction of Travel

Tail Walk

Inverted Tailslap
(UPSLAP)

Fig. 1 Four reinforced novel behaviors, including one shaped behavior, the tailwalk.

The sketches were mounted on index cards and presented in random fashion to each rater separately. A coefficient of concordance (W) of 0.598 was found for agreement between trainers on the ranking of various behaviors; this value is significant at the 0.001 level, indicating a high degree of agreement (Siegel, 1956).

To test the possibility that the trainers were judging complexity rather than novelty in ranking, another questionnaire was prepared requesting ranking according to relative degree of complexity of action. Because some of the original group of 12 trainers were unavailable for retesting, the questionnaire was presented to a group of 49 naive students. The coefficient of concordance (W) for agreement between students was $+0.295$, significant at the 0.001 level. When the rankings for complexity and frequency were contrasted for each behavior, it was found that some agreement existed between the scores given by the two rating groups, Spearman Rank Correlation (RHO) $+0.54$, significant at the 0.05 level.

Thus, there seems to be some agreement between complexity and frequency, which should be expected, since complex behaviors require more muscle expenditure than simple ones. Furthermore, analysis was biased by the fact that the experienced group was asked to rate all behaviors serially, and had no way other than complexity to rate the several behaviors which many of them stated they had never seen. However, the agreement between complexity and frequency was not as large between groups as it was within groups; allowing for the fact that the use of two rating groups makes it impossible to generalize the rating comparisons in a strict sense, the low frequency assigned to some non-complex behaviors by the experienced group suggests that complexity and novelty are not necessarily positively correlated.

RESULTS

Sessions 1 to 14

In the first session, Hou was admitted into the experimental tank and, when given no commands, breached. Breaching, or jumping into the air and coming down sideways, is a normal action in a porpoise. This response was reinforced, and the animal began to repeat it on an average of four times a minute for 8 min. Toward the end of the 9-min session it porpoised, or leaped smoothly out of the water and in, once or twice. It continued to breach in the absence of the trainer, during a half-hour break. In the second session porpoising was reinforced and was repeated several times.

Hou began the third session by porpoising; when this behavior was not reinforced, the animal rapidly developed a behavior pattern of porpoising in front of the trainer, entering the water in an inverted position, turning right side up, swimming in a large circle, and returning to porpoise in front of the trainer again. It did this 25 times without interruption over a period of 12.5 min. Finally, it stopped and laid its head against the pool edge at the trainer's feet. This behavior, nicknamed "beaching", was reinforced and repeated (Fig. 2).

Sessions 5, 6, and 7 followed the same pattern. Hou

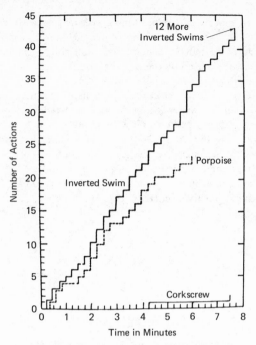

Fig. 2 Cumulative record of Session 7, a typical early session, in which the porpoise began emitting the previously reinforced response. This response gradually extinguished when another response was reinforced.

began each session with the behavior that had been reinforced in the previous session. Occasionally this behavior was chosen for reinforcement when the trainer felt it had not been strongly established in the previous session. If the first response was not reinforced, Hou ran through its repertoire of responses reinforced in previous sessions: breaching, porpoising, beaching, and swimming upsidedown. If no reinforcement was forthcoming, it took up the rigid pattern of porpoising, inverting, circling.

The trainers decided to shape specific responses in order to interrupt Hou's unvarying repetition of a limited repertoire. Session 8 was devoted to shaping a "tail walk", or the behavior of balancing vertically half out of the water. The tail walk was reinforced in Session 9, and Sessions 10 and 11 were devoted to shaping a "tail wave", the response of lifting the tail from the water. The tail wave was emitted and reinforced in Session 12.

While this represented a departure from the primary goal of conditioning novel behavior, the experimenters realized that Malia, the show animal, had experienced some training sessions in which, no new spontaneous action being emitted, some specific response was shaped. It was not known whether or not the shaping sessions had contributed to Malia's ability to emit novel responses. Therefore, the inclusion of shaping in Hou's training seemed permissible. It also seemed desirable to prevent a low level of reinforcement from leading to extinction of all responses.

At the end of Session 10, Hou slapped its tail twice, which was reinforced but not repeated. At the end of Session 12, Hou departed from the stereotyped pattern to the extent of inverting, turning right-side up, and then inverting again while circling. The experimenters observed and reinforced this underwater revolution from a distance, while leaving the experimental area.

Although a weekend then intervened, Hou began Session 13 by swimming in the inverted position, then right-side-up, then inverted again. This behavior, dubbed a "corkscrew", was reinforced, and by means of an increasing variable ratio, was extended to five complete revolutions per reinforcement. In Session 14, the experimenters rotated their positions, and reinforced any descent by the animal toward the bottom of the tank, in a further effort not only to expand Hou's repertoire but also to interrupt the persistent circling behavior.

Sessions 15 and 16

The next morning, as the experimenters set up their equipment, Hou was unusually active in the holding tank. It slapped its tail twice, and this was so unusual that the trainer reinforced the response in the holding tank. When Session 15 began, Hou emitted the response reinforced in the previous session, of swimming near the bottom, and then the response previous to that of the corkscrew, and then fell into the habitual circling and porpoising, with, however, the addition of a tail-slap on re-entering the water. This slap was reinforced, and the animal then combined slapping with breaching, and then began slapping disassociated from jumping; for the first time it emitted responses in all parts of the tank, rather than right in front of the trainer. The 10-min session ended when 17 tailslaps had been reinforced, and other non-reinforced responses had dropped out.

Session 16 began after a 10-min break. Hou became extremely active when the trainer appeared and immediately offered twisting breaches, landing on its belly and its back. It also began somersaulting on its long axis in mid-air. The trainer began reinforcing the last, a "flip", common in the genus *Stenella* but not normally seen in *Steno*, and Hou became very active, swimming in figure eights (unprecedented) and leaping repeatedly. The flip occurred 44 times, intermingled with some of the previously reinforced responses and with three other responses that had not been seen before: an upside-down tailslap, a side-swipe with the tail, and an aerial spin on the short axis of the body (see Fig. 3).

The previous maximum number of types of responses offered in a single session was five. The average number of types was less than two per session. At no time before Session 16 was more than one new behavior seen, and in all but three cases—breaching, beaching, and porpoising—the new behavior was at least partly developed by the trainer. In Session 16, Hou emitted a total of eight behaviors, each one many times, including four completely new, unreinforced behaviors, two of which, the spin and the flip, were elaborately performed from the beginning.

This session also differed from previous ones in that once the flip had become established, the other behaviors did not tend to drop out. After 24 min, the varied activity—tailslaps, breaches, sidewipes with the tail, and the new behavior of spinning in the air—occurred more rather than less frequently, until the session was brought to a close by the trainer. The previous maximum number of responses in a given session was 110 (in Session 9, a 31-min session). In Session 16, Hou emitted 192 responses in a 23-min session, an everage of 8.3

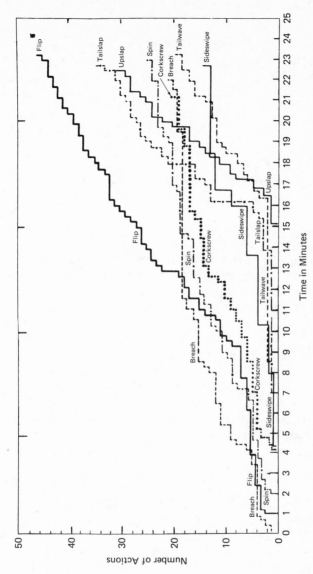

Fig. 3 Cumulative record of Session 16, in which the porpoise emitted eight different types of responses, four of which were novel (flip, spin, sideswipe, and upslap).

responses per min compared to a previous maximum average of 3.6 responses per min.

By Session 16, the experimenters had apparently been successful in establishing a class of responses characterized by the description, "only new kinds of responses will be reinforced", and consequently the porpoise was emitting an extensive variety of new responses. The differences between Session 16 and previous sessions may be seen by comparing the cumulative record for Session 16 (Fig. 3) with that of Session 7, a typical earlier session (Fig. 2).

Sessions 17 to 27

In Sessions 17 to 27, the new types of responses emitted in Session 16 were selected, one by one, for reinforcement, and some old responses were reinforced again so that they could be photographed. Other new responses, such as unclassifiable twisting jumps, and sinking head downwards, occurred sporadically. The average rate of response and the numbers of types of responses per session remained more than twice as high as pre-Session 16 levels.

Hou's general activity changed in two other ways after Session 16. First, if no reinforcement occurred in a period of several minutes, the rate and level of activity declined but the animal did not necessarily resume a stereotyped behavior pattern. Secondly, the animal's activity now included much behavior typically associated in cetaceans with situations producing frustration or aggressiveness, such as slapping the water with head, tail, pectoral fin, or whole body (Burgess, 1968).

Sessions 28 to 33

In all of the final sessions, the criterion that the behavior must be a new one was enforced. A new behavior that had been seen but not reinforced previously, the inverted tailslap, had been reinforced in Session 27. Session 28 began with a variety of responses, including another that had been seen but not reinforced before, a sideswipe at water surface with the tail, which was reinforced. In Session 29, Hou's activity included an inverted leap that fulfilled the criterion (Fig. 4). In Session 30, Hou offered 60 responses over a period of 15 min, none of which were considered new, and were not therefore reinforced.

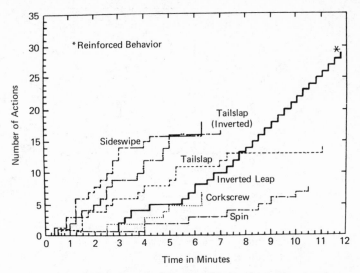

Fig. 4 Cumulative record of Session 29, in which the porpoise emitted the three most recently reinforced responses initially, but soon emitted a novel response. When this response was reinforced, the other extinguished.

In Sessions 31, 32, and 33, held the next day, Hou's behavior was more completely controlled by the criteria that only new types of responses were reinforced and that only one type of response was reinforced per session. In Session 31, Hou entered the tank and, after a preliminary jump, stood on its tail and clapped its jaws at the trainer, who, taken by surprise, failed to reinforce the maneuver. Hou then emitted a brief series of leaps and then executed a backwards aerial flip that was reinforced and immediately repeated 14 times without intervening responses of other types. In Session 32, after one porpoise and one flip, Hou executed an upside-down porpoise, and, after it was reinforced, repeated this new response 10 times, again without other responses (Figs. 5, 6).

In the third session of the day, Hou did not initially emit a response judged new by the observers. After 10 min and 72 responses of variable types, the rate of response declined to 1 per min and then gradually rose again to seven responses per minute after 19 min. No reinforcements occurred during this period. At the end of 19 min, Hou stood on its tail and

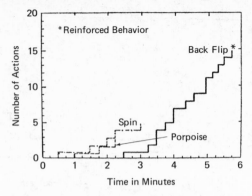

Fig. 5 Cumulative record of Session 31. The porpoise emitted a novel response early in the session, and other responses extinguished immediately when the novel response was reinforced.

clapped its jaws, spitting water towards the trainer; this time the action was reinforced, and was repeated five times.

Hou had now produced a new behavior in six out of seven consecutive sessions. In Sessions 31 and 32, Hou furthermore began each session with a new response and emitted no unreinforceable responses once reinforcement was presented. This establishment of a series of new types of responses was considered to be the conclusion of the experiment.

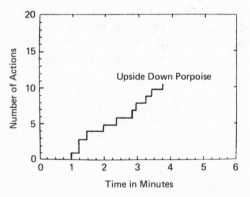

Fig. 6 Cumulative record of Session 32. The porpoise emitted only a novel response in this session.

DISCUSSION

Over a period of 4 yr since Sea Life Park and the neighboring Oceanic Institute were opened, the training staff has observed and trained over 50 cetaceans of seven different species. Of the 16 behaviors reinforced in this experiment, five (breaching, porpoising, inverted swimming, tail slap, sideswipe) have been observed to occur spontaneously in every species; four (beaching, tailwalk, inverted tail slap, spitting) have been developed by shaping in various animals but very rarely occur spontaneously in any; three (spinning, back porpoise, forward flip) occur spontaneously only in one species of *Stenella* and have never been observed at Sea Life Park in other species; and four (corkscrew, back flip, tailwave, inverted leap) have never been observed to occur spontaneously. While this does not imply that these behaviors do not sometimes occur spontaneously, whatever the species, it does serve to indicate that a single animal, in emitting these 16 types of responses, would be engaging in behavior well outside the species norm.

A technique of reinforcing a series of different, normally occurring actions, in a series of training sessions, did therefore serve, in the case of Hou, as with Malia, to establish in the animal a highly increased probability that new types of behavior would be emitted.

j This ability to emit an unusual response need not be regarded as an example of cleverness peculiar to the porpoise. It is possible that the same technique could be used to achieve a similar result with pigeons. If a different, normally occurring action in a pigeon is reinforced each day for a series of days, until the normal repertoire (turning, pecking, flapping wings, *etc.*) is exhausted, the pigeon may come to emit novel responses difficult to produce even by shaping.

k A similar process may be involved in one traditional system of the training of five-gaited show horses, which perform at three natural gaits, the walk, trot, and canter, and two artificial gaits, the slow-gait and the rack. The trainer first reinforces the performance of the natural gaits and brings this performance under stimulus control. The discriminative stimuli, which control not only the gait, but also speed, direction, and position of the horse while executing the gait, consist of pressure and release from the rider's legs, pressures on the reins and consequently the bit, shifting of weight in the saddle, and sometimes signals with whip and voice. To elicit the artificial gait, the trainer next presents the animal with a new group of stimuli, shaking the bit back and forth in the horse's mouth and vibrating the legs against the horse's sides, while preventing the animal from terminating the stimuli **k** (negative reinforcement) by means of the previously reinforced responses of walking, trotting, or cantering. The animal will emit a variety of responses that eventually may include the pattern of stepping, novel to the horse though familiar to the trainer, called the rack (Hildebrand, 1965). The pattern, however brief, is reinforced, and once established is extended in duration and brought under stimulus control. (The slow-gait is derived from the rack by shaping.)

Upon conclusion of this experiment, Hou was returned to the care of Sea Life Park trainers and introduced as a performer in five daily shows six days a week until the time of writing (April, 1969). Hou performs a number of behaviors under stimulus control, some of which first appeared during this experiment. Spitting, for example, is now offered in response to the discriminative stimulus of a hand signal, and, as is the case for all conditioned behaviors used for performance, has been successfully extinguished in the absence of the stimulus. The trend towards the emission of novel behavior has, in the case of both Hou and Malia, been reversed during normal training and performance; they respond to learned stimuli correctly, with no more than normal unconditioned activity, and a single new response can be reinforced and shaped with no great increase occurring in types of responses offered. However, both animals can be stimulated to a high rate of activity, including novel behavior, if the trainer leaves the normal demonstration training platform and takes up position across the tank in the station used during the experiment. Thus, a session of reinforcing novel behavior can be introduced occasionally into a show without interfering with the normal presentation of behaviors under stimulus control. This occurs perhaps once a month. At least one behavior—flapping the last third of the body in the air, while hanging head down in the water—has been first reinforced, later to be brought under stimulus control, during such a session.

Comparison may be made here between this work and that of Maltzman (1960). Working in the formidably rich matrix of human subjects and verbal behavior, Maltzman described a successful procedure for eliciting original responses, consisting of reinforcing different responses to the same stimuli, essentially the same procedure followed with Hou and Malia. It is interesting to note that behavior considered by the authors to indicate anger in the porpoise was observed under similar circumstances in human subjects by Maltzman: "An impression gained from observing Ss in the experimental situation is that repeated evocation of different responses to the same stimuli becomes quite frustrating; Ss are disturbed by what quickly becomes a surprisingly difficult task. This disturbed behavior indicates that the procedure may not be trivial and does approximate a non-laboratory situation involving originality or inventiveness, with its frequent concomitant frustration."

Maltzman also found that eliciting and reinforcing original behavior in one set of circumstances increased the tendency for original responses in other kinds of situations, which seems likewise to be true for Hou and Malia. Hou continues to exhibit a marked increase in general level of activity. Hou has learned to leap tank partitions to gain access to other porpoises, a skill very seldom developed by a captive porpoise. When a trainer was occupied at an adjoining porpoise tank Malia jumped from the water, skidded across 6 ft of wet pavement, and tapped the trainer on the ankle with its rostrum or snout, a truly bizarre act for an entirely aquatic animal.

Maltzman also observed that under some conditions originality may be increased by evoking a relatively large number of different responses to different stimuli. The confirmation of this hypothesis is suggested by our informal observations of performing cetaceans, at least some of which develop a tendency to original behavior after a year or two of reinforcement with respect to many different kinds of stimuli and responses. We do not observe this "sophistication" developing in animals that are trained with respect to one group of responses and stimuli and then continue in the same pattern, however complex, for months or years.

Individual differences in the ability to create unorthodox responses no doubt exist; Malia's novel responses, judged *in toto*, are more spectacular and "imaginative" than Hou's. However, by using the technique of training for novelty described herein, it should be possible to induce a tendency towards spontaneity and creative or unorthodox response in most individuals of a broad range of species.

REFERENCES

Burgess, K. The behavior and training of a Killer Whale at San Diego Sea World. *International Zoo Yearbook*, 1968, *8*, 202–205.

Hildebrand, M. Symmetrical gaits of horses. *Science*, 1965, *150*, 701–708.

Maltzman, I. On the training of originality. *Psychological Review*, 1960, *67*, 229–242.

Norris, K. S. Open ocean diving test with a trained porpoise (*Steno bredanensis*). *Deep Sea Research*, 1965, *12*, 505–509.

Siegel, S. *Nonparametric statistics for the behavioral sciences*. New York: McGraw-Hill, 1956.

Skinner, B. F. Two synthetic social relations. *Journal of the Experimental Analysis of Behavior*, 1962, *5*, 531–533.

CASE ANALYSIS

Two models of learning have dominated the research activities of learning psychologists during the early part of this century. One model was developed by Ivan Pavlov and is commonly called classical conditioning; the other model was suggested by E. L. Thorndike and refined by B. F. Skinner and is referred to as operant conditioning. The initial experiments of both groups attempted to identify the conditions for learning using infra-human subjects. Pavlov used his famous salivating dogs while Thorndike studied the effects of reward on the behavior of cats. Skinner employed rats in his early experiments and then pigeons and finally, among other species, humans. The contemporary period has seen a great proliferation of species used in the learning laboratory, all with the basic purpose to establish laws of behavior. The use of a porpoise in the present study is a logical step to illustrate the effectiveness of operant conditioning in yet another species.

The model developed by B. F. Skinner has several basic components which the authors of the "The Creative Porpoise" have skillfully applied. As you read this experiment try to identify some of the following principles of operant behavior.

An important principle of operant conditioning is that responses which are followed by a reward or positive reinforcement tend to increase, while nonrewarded responses tend to decrease. Skinner demonstrated this principle in rats by measuring the increase in bar pressing responses which were followed by reward. The apparatus developed by Skinner has been described previously and it is suggested that you refer back to Chapter 2 for better understanding of this article. The initial behavior of a rat placed in a "Skinner box" is normally exploratory in nature; he sniffs the corner, moves from one side to the other, examines the walls, and washes his face. Only a small number of these responses have anything to do with the response of bar press. The skilled researcher can identify preparatory bar pressing responses and reinforce them. The process of selectively reinforcing successive approximations of the principal response (bar pressing) is called shaping. Gradually the animal moves closer to the bar, then places his paw close to the bar, touches it, and eventually depresses it.

Much information has been collected regarding the specific conditions which facilitate operant conditioning. For example, if the reward is presented immediately after the appropriate response, then conditioning is more rapid than if the reward is delayed. In reading the article by Pryor et al., notice how they try to present the reinforcement as soon after the response to be conditioned as was practical.

Other researchers have studied the role that secondary reinforcers (stimuli which have been associated with the primary reward) have on behavior. The general conclusions of these studies is that secondary reinforcers have strong rewarding properties. Consider the reward properties of the secondary reinforcement of money in many societies. In this study Pryor et al. use a distinguishable signal (a whistle) as a conditioned reinforcer.

The results of operant conditioning experiments lend themselves to graphic representation in the form of a cumulative frequency record. On a cumulative frequency graph, the subject's responses are accumulated and scaled on the ordinate while time is recorded on the abscissa. Since the responses are accumulative, the response curve never goes down; nonresponding is depicted as a line parallel to the abscissa.

This article was selected to illustrate not only the principles of operant behavior but also to give the student a look at an experiment which is largely descriptive in nature. You will note that only one subject was used and the statistical portion of the paper is brief. Most research in psychology depends on large samples; however, to infer that psychological research must study large samples in order to be valid is an unwarranted conclusion. Pryor, Haag, and O'Reilly describe the learning process with clarity by thoroughly examining the behavior of a single subject.

REVIEW

Other articles used in this book began with a review of other studies. Pryor, Haag, and O'Reilly introduce their paper with a general statement of the use of operant conditioning in a variety of species (a). In the following two paragraphs they describe some natural observations which led to the hypothesis (b) and an abbreviated statement of their method (c). It is important to note that the development of an hypothesis may emanate from many sources. Although the most frequent source of an hypothesis is previous research, another significant source is the observation of behavior in a natural setting.

METHOD

Paragraphs (d), (e), and (f) contain the identification of the subject, a description of how conditioning was done, and an explanation of the technique used to record the data. In paragraph (e) the authors describe the use of a bell which was sounded at the beginning of the training session (see underlined passage). The use of a signal at the outset of an experiment is called a discriminative stimulus and it sets the occasion for the conditioned operant. The bell in this experiment signified to Hou that it was time for him to do his thing.

This paper may appear to be an observational study rather than an empirical experiment. Upon closer observation it is apparent that there are independent and dependent variables, operational definition of terms, hypothesis testing, controlled conditions, and a comparison group to name but a few of the characteristics of experimentation.

This experiment differs from several other experiments reviewed below because the dependent variable (novel behavior) is followed by the independent variable (reinforcement). Compare this sequence with Terkel and Rosenblatt's article "Maternal Behavior Induced by Maternal Blood Plasma Injected into Virgin rats" (p. 118) in which the dependent variable (maternal behavior) is *preceded* by the independent variable (maternal blood plasma). You may have observed in the Pryor *et al.* article that the porpoise's behavior and reinforcement was ongoing and it could be argued that a chain of responses—reinforcement-response, reinforcement-response would develop. The sequence of independent-dependent variable then becomes a matter of deciding which came first: the reinforcement or the behavior.

Several statements in paragraph (**f**) require comment. The researchers are careful to have two observers who tape record their observations which were then transcribed into a typed manuscript. They also have a precise copy of the time and frequency of the conditioned reinforcer (a whistle).

In (**g**) an operational definition of a reinforceable act is stated. In shaping behavior the act to be reinforced is sometimes ambiguous and some researchers will "play it by ear," i.e., they will make a decision to reinforce or not reinforce on the basis of ongoing behavior. Since scientific procedure must be specified in sufficient detail to allow the experiment to be exactly replicated, Pryor *et al.* attempt to reduce the ambiguity of shaping by operationally defining reinforceable responses. In (**h**) they explain the measure of experimental reliability used.

A final procedural question is raised in (**i**) and some evidence is presented in answer to the question. Complexity of responses rather than novelty of responses may have been conditioned. The experimenters used a form of consentual validation in which observations made by one experimenter are compared with observations of another experimenter to resolve the issue.

RESULTS

The results reported in this article are generally self-explanatory, and it is suggested you thoroughly read the original transcript. Several general remarks may guide your reading.

First, you will notice the absence of F tests or t tests. Indeed the paper is noticeably lacking in statistical analyses. In lieu of such analysis the writers present a well-documented protocol of the changing behavior of the porpoise. Finally, the use of cumulative frequency graphs is skillfully utilized in this article. Pryor *et al.* provide a daily graph (Figs. 2 to 6) in which the porpoise's behavior is charted using the coordinates of responses (vertical axis) and time (horizontal axis).

It is important for you to study these graphs as they are used as the primary source of results. In Fig. 2 there are three distinct components: (1) the number of actions, (2) time in minutes, and (3) behavior (inverted swim, porpoise, and cork screw). Notice the relationship between the three behaviors and how the inverted swim rapidly increases. The same three components are in Fig. 3 and numerous other behavior characteristics are observed. Trace the development of the flip in Fig. 3.

DISCUSSION

The implication of training creative behavior in the porpoise is discussed in relationship to achieving similar results with the pigeon (**j**) and the horse (**k**), and possible common features of the present study and previous work by Maltzman are suggested (**l**).

QUESTIONS

1.   In this study identify:

conditioned reinforcer
discriminative stimulus
operant
drive

cumulative frequency graph
shaping
creativity—operational definition
response-reinforcement latency

2.   Can you suggest another technique for measuring the responses?

3.   Take another species—e.g., dog, goldfish, squirrel—and write a reinforcement schedule for the training of novel behavior. Operationally define your terms.

4. Write a brief essay describing the worthwhileness of naturalistic observations.

5. Write a lesson plan for 6-year-old children in which creative reactions are shaped and reinforced. What limitations to your lessons do you see?

9

MATERNAL BEHAVIOR

MATERNAL BEHAVIOR INDUCED BY MATERNAL BLOOD PLASMA INJECTED INTO VIRGIN RATS

Joseph Terkel, *Institute of Animal Behavior*
Jay S. Rosenblatt, *Rutgers University*

Induction of maternal behavior (i.e., retrieving) in virgins by exposure to young pups was studied to investigate effects of blood plasma from a post-parturient female. Control groups were injected with blood plasma from nonmaternal females in proestrus and diestrus phases of the vaginal estrous cycle and with saline solution. Virgins injected with maternal blood plasma had significantly shorter latencies of maternal behavior than other groups. Injections of saline and proestrus blood plasma had no effect on maternal behavior. Virgins injected with diestrus blood plasma were significantly delayed in displaying maternal behavior. The findings indicate that there is a humoral basis for the appearance of maternal behavior after parturition.[1]

Several recent attempts to induce maternal behavior in the rat by means of various hormones (i.e., estrogen, proges-

Reprinted by permission from *Journal of Comparative and Physiological Psychology*, 1968, *65* (3), 479–482. Published by the American Psychological Association.

[1] This research was supported by National Institute of Mental Health Research Grant MH-08604 to J. S. R. and Biological Medicine Grant FR-7059 to J. T. We wish to thank D. S. Lehrman and B. Sachs for reading the manuscript. Publication No. 50 from the Institute of Animal Behavior, Rutgers University, Newark.

terone, and prolactin) injected directly into virgin or experienced females have not yielded results that would increase our understanding of the hormonal basis of this behavior (Beach & Wilson, 1963; Lott, 1962; Lott & Fuchs, 1962). In this laboratory injected hormones (prolactin and oxytocin) have failed also to maintain maternal behavior in females that have become maternal after parturition or have been made maternal by Caesarean-section delivery of their fetuses several days before parturition. However, the conviction that maternal behavior in the rat is based upon hormones is supported by the success in inducing nest building in the mouse with progesterone (Koller, 1952, 1955) and in the hamster with estrogen and progesterone (Richards, 1965). Some success has been reported in inducing maternal nest building in rabbits using a combination of hormones (e.g., stilbestrol, progesterone, and prolactin were used by Zarrow, Sawin, Ross, & Denenberg, 1962).

a   In view of the difficulty of inducing maternal behavior in female rats with injected hormones, a difficulty no doubt based upon failure to introduce either the proper hormone or hormones in the proper order and dose level, we have attempted a different approach to the problem. Remaining close to the natural conditions under which maternal behavior normally appears at and shortly after parturition, we have attempted to transfer blood plasma from postparturient females that have become maternal within the past 48 hr. to virgins, hoping thereby to induce maternal behavior in the latter. Establishing that maternal blood plasma carries a substance or substances

b   capable of inducing maternal behavior in virgins would be a first step in identifying the humoral basis of maternal behavior.

We have shown recently that virgin females can be induced to show maternal behavior when they are exposed to young pups continuously for about 5 days (Rosenblatt, 1967). Cosnier (1963) reported a similar finding using shorter daily exposures. Both studies confirm an early suggestion by Wiesner and Sheard (1933) which was only partially verified in their own studies. Maternal behavior induced under these conditions appears to be of nonhormonal origin since ovariectomizing or hypophysectomizing virgins before exposing them to pups did not prevent the appearance of maternal behavior or alter, significantly, latencies for the onset of a major item of maternal behavior, namely retrieving (Cosnier & Couterier, 1966; Rosenblatt, 1967). In this study, therefore, we observed whether the latency for the appearance of retrieving (and other items of maternal behavior) by virgins exposed to young pups was significantly reduced by prior injection of maternal blood plasma as compared to prior injection of blood plasma taken from virgins in the proestrus or diestrus phases of the vaginal estrous cycle, or prior injection of saline solution.

c

METHOD

Subjects.   Thirty-two virgin females, 60 days of age at the start of the experiment, were obtained from Charles River Breeding Farm, Dover, Mass. Twenty-four additional Ss of the same age provided blood plasma for the injections. Other rats provided the pups used in the maternal behavior tests. The Ss were housed individually in 18 × 20 × 16½-in. rectangular cages, each with transparent Plexiglas walls, grid floor, wall feeder, water bottle, and two bins containing hay and coarse wood shavings for nesting material. They were fed Purina chow and water ad lib supplemented twice weekly with vitamin-enriched bread, carrots, and lettuce.

The Ss were divided into four equal-sized groups. One group received plasma taken from maternal Ss; injections were given when Ss were in various unspecified phases of the vaginal estrous cycle. One control group consisted of Ss in proestrus that received plasma taken from females that were also in proestrus, and a second control group consisted of Ss in diestrus that received plasma taken from females that were also in diestrus. The fourth group of Ss received an injection of .9 percent saline solution at various unspecified phases of the vaginal estrous cycle.

Procedures.   Blood was withdrawn from the donors within 48 hr. after parturition, after it was clearly established that these Ss were performing maternal behavior normally. Blood taken from estrous-cycling donors was withdrawn within 1 hr. after the vaginal smear indicated either proestrus or diestrus. Between 6–8 cc of blood was withdrawn from the heart. To withdraw the blood, the donors were anesthetized with ether, and the heart was surgically exposed by a chest incision to one side of the midline. The blood was withdrawn using a 1½-in. 16-gauge needle with a 20-cc syringe containing 15–20 units of Heparin Sodium to prevent blood clotting.

About 4 min. elapsed from the time the donor was judged to be completely anesthetized until the blood was first transferred from the syringe to a test tube and centrifuging was started. When a zone of clear plasma, free of blood cells, appeared 3–4 cc of plasma was drawn into a 5-cc syringe and injected into an S with a $\frac{1}{2}$-in. 27-gauge needle. Plasma injection was completed in 4 min. Each experimental S received all of its plasma from a single donor female.

The S was lightly anesthetized with ether, a small incision was made on the inner surface of the upper thigh, and the right femoral vein was exposed. The needle was inserted into the vein, a small amount of blood was withdrawn, and then the plasma (or saline solution) was injected slowly over a period of $2\frac{1}{2}$ min. The incision was closed with wound clips. In this inbred strain of rats, plasma transfer between any two strain mates does not result in anaphylactic shock.

Maternal Behavior Tests. Each animal was given a 15-min. retrieving test 1 hr. before blood was withdrawn from the proestrus and diestrus donors and plasma or saline was injected into the recipient Ss. Since no S retrieved during this test it was not necessary to eliminate any of them from the experiment.

Tests following the injection of either plasma or saline were begun after it was judged that Ss were fully recovered from the anesthetic used during the injection. Each S was judged to be recovered if it was able to walk around the edge of a bell jar maintaining its balance; if it fell from the edge it was retested at a later time. It was possible for the first postinjection test to begin in all Ss 1 hr. after the injection since all Ss were fully recovered from the ether about 5 min. after the injection.

Five pups, 5–10 days of age, were placed at the front of each Ss cage. Retrieving was observed for 15 min., following which observations for 1-min. periods at 20-min. intervals were made over the next 2 hr. During the 1-min. period of observation the occurrence of retrieving, crouching over the young, licking the young, nest building, and other maternal and nonmaternal items of behavior were recorded. Nesting material had previously been spread over the floor. At the end of the 2-hr. test the pups were left with Ss until the next morning at which time they were removed and replaced by a fresh litter of five pups in the same age range. The test procedure was repeated daily until an S retrieved pups in two consecutive daily tests. Since retrieving is usually the last item of maternal behavior to appear when pups are used to induce it, all Ss had already shown the other main items of maternal behavior (i.e., crouching over young, licking young, nest building) by the termination of testing.

Several *S*s that had been injected with maternal plasma were observed continually on the first day following the first test to see if items of maternal behavior would appear between the first and the second test, 22 hr. later.

RESULTS

d Mean latencies in days for the onset of retrieving for the various groups, shown in Table 1, indicate that plasma taken from a lactating mother within 48 hr. after delivery is capable of inducing a more rapid maternal response to pups than saline and either proestrus or diestrus plasma ($F = 9.79$, $df = 3/28$, $p < .01$; data transformed to square roots). Under the combined influence of maternal plasma and stimulation from pups, retrieving appeared in an average of 2 days. This time was significantly shorter than when saline or proestrus plasma was injected or when diestrus plasma was injected (Duncan's New Multiple Range test at the .05 level). Proestrus plasma combined with the proestrus condition of the recipient virgin was similar in its effect on maternal behavior to saline but diestrus plasma given to females in diestrus produced a significant delay in the mean latency for the onset of retrieving (Duncan's New Multiple Range test at the .05 level).

In a previous study (Rosenblatt, 1967) it was established that maternal behavior (i.e., retrieving and other items) can be induced in virgins by exposure to pups, without any prior

Table 1 Mean Latencies in Days for the Onset of Retrieving

GROUP	N	MEAN	SE
Maternal plasma	8	2.25	.97
Proestrus plasma	8	4.62	1.21
Diestrus plasma	8	7.00	2.96
Saline	8	4.00	1.41
Untreated[a]	14	5.79	2.69

[a]Taken from Rosenblatt (1967).

injection, with an average latency of 5.79 ± 2.69 days.[2] The saline-injected proestrus plasma- and diestrus plasma-injected Ss of the present study had average latencies which did not differ significantly from Ss in the earlier study (Mann-Whitney $U = 40$–42, $p > .10$). The average latency of the maternal plasma-injected Ss was, however, significantly shorter than that of the Ss that were only exposed to pups (Mann-Whitney $U = 20$, $p = .02$).

The onset of retrieving was accompanied in all groups by the occurrence of the three other main items of maternal behavior (i.e., crouching over the young, licking, and nest building). With pups continuously present, the onset of an item of maternal behavior, and particularly the onset of retrieving, was followed by its appearance from then on in each of the subsequent daily tests.

Observations of the Ss between the first and second tests led us to believe that the maternal plasma induced maternal behavior more rapidly than our formal test procedure was capable of detecting. Several Ss that were injected with maternal plasma began to show maternal behavior in attenuated fashion within 4–8 hr. after the injection and the beginning of exposure to pups, although, several hours earlier, during the first scheduled test of maternal behavior, they were indifferent to the pups. Two of these were fully maternal, according to our criteria for the virgins, by the second test which was begun 1 day after the injection. Others were not fully maternal until the third test was begun 2 days after the injection.

DISCUSSION

Our study established for the first time that substances carried in the plasma of the newly maternal rat are capable of increasing the readiness of virgins to respond maternally to pups. We have, therefore, finally found a way of accomplishing what Stone (1925) set out to do when he joined in parabiosis

[2] This value differs by -1 day from the published value (Rosenblatt, 1967). In the present study the first test of maternal behavior, performed at the time that pups were first introduced, is called Day 0 while in the previous study it was called Day 1.

a maternal and nonmaternal rat hoping that blood-borne substances responsible for maternal behavior in the former would induce maternal behavior in the latter. Were it not for the failure of these substances to cross from the maternal to the nonmaternal animal, because of selective transmission across the parabiotic union, Stone would have demonstrated what we have found, and perhaps the effect would have been stronger with the continuous exchange of blood that he attempted.

f | The present study does not enable us to identify the substance or substances that are responsible for increasing the maternal responsiveness of the virgins or to determine whether these substances act on the virgin via the endocrine system or directly upon the nervous system. Initially we thought that dividing our plasma control group into two groups, one receiving pro- and the other diestrus plasma, the virgins themselves being in the corresponding phases of the estrous cycle, would enable us to make a first step in identifying the active substances. To the extent that the diestrus blood plasma combined with the diestrus condition of the recipient virgin produced a delay in the onset of maternal behavior we have been partially successful. However, any identification of ovarian hormones or pituitary secretions as the active substances would be highly speculative and incapable of substantiation at this time. Our findings therefore await further analysis of hormonal secretions during the estrous cycle, pregnancy, and parturition.

An added finding of importance does emerge from this study which was surprising to us. Our previous work indicated that maternal responsiveness increases gradually during pregnancy (Lott & Rosenblatt, 1967), and we interpreted this as indicating that the hormonal conditions during pregnancy gradually sensitized the neural substrate of maternal behavior thereby preparing for the appearance of maternal behavior at parturition. The present study suggests that there need be no prolonged period (i.e., 22 days of pregnancy) of sensitization for substances contained in maternal plasma to have their effect on maternal behavior. It would appear that the gradual increase in maternal responsiveness which we found during pregnancy after Caesarean-section deliveries (Lott & Rosenblatt, 1967) need not be built up by a continual addition of "units" of maternal responsiveness. Rather the level of maternal responsiveness at each period of pregnancy reflects for that particular moment the current capability of the blood to stimulate maternal behavior and this capability presumably undergoes a continuous increase until it is fully established around parturition. In this respect then our findings agree with those of Moltz and Wiener (1966) and Denenberg, Grota, and Zarrow (1963) that hormonal secretions at parturition are likely to be important for the induction of maternal behavior.

REFERENCES

Beach, F. A., & Wilson, J. R. Effects of prolactin, progesterone, and estrogen on reactions of nonpregnant rats to foster young. *Psychol. Rep.*, 1963, *13*, 231–239.

Cosnier, J. Quelques problèmes posés par le "comportement maternal provoqué" chez la ratte. *CR Soc. Biol.*, *Paris*, 1963, *157*, 1611–1613.

Cosnier, J., & Couterier, C. Comportement maternal provoqué chez les rattes adultes castrées. *CR Soc. Biol.*, *Paris*, 1966, *160*, 789–791.

Denenberg, V. H., Grota, L. J., & Zarrow, M. X. Maternal behavior in the rat: Analysis of cross-fostering. *J. Reprod. Fertil.*, 1963, *5*, 133–141.

Koller, G. Der Nestbau der Weiber Mause and seine hormonale Auslosung. *Verh. dtsch. zool. Ges.*, *Freiberg*, 1952, 160–168.

Koller, G. Hormonale und psychische Steuerung beim Nestbau Weiber Mause. *Zool. Anz.*, *(Suppl.)*, 1955, *19*, 125–132.

Lott, D. F. The role of progesterone in the maternal behavior of rodents. *J. comp. physiol. Psychol.*, 1962, *55*, 610–613.

Lott, D. F., & Fuchs, S. S. Failure to induce retrieving by sensitization or the injection of prolactin. *J. comp. physiol. Psychol.*, 1962, *55*, 1111–1113.

Lott, D. F., & Rosenblatt, J. S. Development of maternal responsiveness during pregnancy in the rat. In B. M. Foss (Ed.), *Determinants of infant behaviour IV*. London: Methuen, 1967

Moltz, H., & Weiner, E. Effects of ovariectomy on maternal behavior of primiparous and multiparous rats. *J. comp. physiol. Psychol.*, 1966, *62*, 382–387.

Richards, M. P. M. Aspects of maternal behaviour in the golden hamster. Unpublished doctoral dissertation, Cambridge University, 1965.

Rosenblatt, J. S. Non-hormonal basis of maternal behavior in the rat. *Science*, 1967, *156*, 1512–1514.

Stone, C. P. Preliminary note on maternal behavior of rats living in parabiosis. *Endocrinology*, 1925, *9*, 505–512.

Wiesner, B. P., & Sheard, N. M. *Maternal behaviour in the rat.* London: Oliver and Boyd, 1933.

Zarrow, M. X., Sawin, P. B., Ross, S., & Denenberg, V. H. Maternal behavior and its endocrine bases in the rabbit. In E. L. Bliss. (Ed.), *Roots of behavior*. New York: Harper, 1962.

CASE ANALYSIS

Maternal behavior (i.e., nest building, care of the young, retrieving, nursing, etc.) has long been considered an "instinct." However, in recent years it has become apparent that calling a behavior an "instinct" tells us little about its causes. Psychologists have therefore begun to carry out studies of the factors underlying such behavior. These factors include stimuli coming from the nest or the young, brain mechanisms, past experience. The suggestion that hormones too may play a role in controlling such behavior comes from the fact that maternal behavior develops very gradually and fades away in the same manner. That is, nest building and the bodily changes accompanying maternity take place prior to birth and disappear gradually as the young grow older. This characteristic of the behavior suggests that it may be related to the gradual buildup and decline of some chemical substance in the blood. One way to demonstrate the involvement of a hormone in the control of a behavior is to inject the hormone and see whether it can induce the behavior. Previous studies of this type have failed to produce clear-cut results and the present study is an attempt to approach the problem in a somewhat different fashion.

This experiment has a distinctive independent variable and a control group. The experimenters measured the reaction of an experimental group against the reaction of a control group. You should note that something was done to the subjects; they were injected with various chemicals.

REVIEW

In the review of literature, Terkel and Rosenblatt carefully present two sides of a controversy surrounding the hormonal basis of maternal behavior. On the one hand, while some researchers have found strong evidence for the hormonal basis of maternal behavior others have not. In (a) the authors speculate about the ambiguity of previous experimental results by suggesting that such studies have not employed the proper hormones in the proper order and at proper dose levels. However, if the blood conditions in virgin rats (presumably behaviorally nonmaternal) were nearly identical to the blood conditions of rats who had recently delivered a litter of pups (presumably behaviorally maternal), then a reliable measure of the serological basis of maternal behavior would be possible. The authors suggest in (b) that we should identify the gross phenomenon of the hormonal basis of maternal behavior as a first step which would presumably lead to a more discrete analysis of specific chemicals responsible for this behavior.

The last sentence of the review (c) contains the hypothesis to be tested and a brief version of the research plan. In effect, the researchers state the dependent variable, latency of retrieving pups, and the independent variables, injection of different groups with (1) maternal blood plasma, (2) blood from animals in the proestrus phase, (3) blood from animals in the diestrus phase, and (4) saline solution. A fifth group was not injected and served as a control. The proestrus phase in rats is the period immediately prior to estrus ("heat") and the diestrus period is the period which follows estrus. Presumably, these phases were selected to reduce the possibility of hormones present during the estrus phase from causing a general increase in the activity level which could have been falsely interpreted as maternal behavior.

METHOD

Three parts are included in this section: the subjects are identified, the procedures are described, and the tests of maternal behavior are specified. In this study, enough detail is present to allow its replication. For example, in describing the subjects the authors identify the breeding farm, age, sex, cage size and construction, feed, water schedule, and nesting material. There is a practical limit to the amount of methodological detail that can be presented. For this reason some items such as temperature, humidity, lighting, etc., are deleted and one could logically infer that these items were controlled.

In the procedure section, Terkel and Rosenblatt demonstrate their considerable talent for unambiguous communication. They explain in detail the method used for blood transfusion. A researcher with some surgical skill could exactly replicate their procedure.

A critical aspect of this study is in the definition of the dependent variable: maternal behavior. The validity of scientific inquiry, to a large extent, rests upon the operational definition of dependent variables and the test of these variables. The present authors suggest several behavioral characteristics that typify maternal behavior, including latency in retrieval of pups, crouching over young, licking young, and nest building.

RESULTS

The essence of this research paper is typified in the first sentence (**d**) of the results section. A main result of this experiment —plasma of lactating rats is capable of inducing more rapid maternal behavior than other substances—is plainly stated. Statistical evidence in the form of the F statistic or analysis of variance is then presented. In addition to the F statistic, the authors employ Duncan's New Multiple Range test and the Mann-Whitney U statistic. Duncan's test is used to ascertain whether significant differences exist between each of the means, while the Mann-Whitney is a special type of analysis for ranked data with two classes of information.

In the second paragraph of the results section the authors introduce an untreated control group from a previous study. This procedure is obviously not as desirable as one which would include an untreated control group within the same experiment. There may be differences between the two experiments in the sample of rats, the handling of the rats, or the experimental procedures. On the other hand, the procedures used in this series of studies is fairly standardized and as such makes a cross-experiment comparison somewhat feasible (although not totally desirable). Data from one experiment should not be analyzed with a second experiment unless the experimenter is quite sure that the subjects and procedures of the two experiments are quite similar.

In the third paragraph of this section the authors introduce some *observational* data which their experimental procedures were not sensitive enough to detect. Observational data of this type is often quite valuable in helping to clarify or further interpret the results. However, it should be noted that data of this type is usually not collected as systematically or precisely as the data collected on the formal testing of the dependent variable. Therefore this type of data should be treated as supplementary to the results found in the formal testing of the dependent variable, and this is how the authors presented it.

DISCUSSION

The discussion of this article begins with a bold statement (**e**) which is a combination of empirically validated evidence and a logically inferred statement. Terkel and Rosenblatt quickly point out that the hypothesis tested in this study is not a new one and, in addition, suggest a reason for previous failures to validate the hypothesis by other research workers. They also state a limitation (**f**) by noting that their study did not specifically identify the substance(s) within the blood responsible for increasing maternal behavior. One can capture a feeling of excitement in this research, and even the beginner to psychology can anticipate the next development.

QUESTIONS

1.   Speculate as to the results if greater quantities of blood had been transfused.

2.   Would you care to make a generalization to human transfusion? Why is this generalization warranted or unwarranted? Do you see any "practical" application of this study?

3.   Why did the authors include a saline group? A proestrus group? A diestrus group? An untreated group?

4.   What significance do you attribute to the results of the diestrus group?

5.   What group(s) would you like to add?

6.   In addition to the behavioral indices of maternal behavior, suggest several physiological measures of maternal tendencies. Could these be quantifiable? Would evaluation of these changes be important to this study? Why? Why not?

7.   This paper might as readily have been published in a physiological journal. What is the relationship between psychology and physiology?

8.   Why are rats used in psychological studies?

10

DEPTH DISCRIMINATION

TWO TYPES OF DEPTH DISCRIMINATION BY THE HUMAN INFANT WITH FIVE INCHES OF VISUAL DEPTH

Richard D. Walk,   *George Washington University*

Infants $6\frac{1}{2}$–15 months of age were tested on the visual cliff with the textured visual surface 5 in. below the glass. Infants were called by the mother from the bisection of shallow and deep sides or from across the deep side. The bisection condition was a threshold in that only 73% of the infants went to the shallow side compared to over 90% at greater visual depths. Most infants could be coaxed across the deep side at 5-in. visual depth, a big change from the 10-in. visual depth, particularly for infants over 10 months of age, few of whom crossed the deep side with 10-in. visual depth.[1]

a

This experiment stemmed from the use of different experimental procedures to investigate depth perception, and thus it is an attempt to resolve questions raised by earlier visual cliff research with the human infant. The early visual cliff research had the mother try to coax the infant across the deep side (Walk & Gibson, 1961). Very few (11 percent) were able to do so. Subsequent research confirmed this finding as long as definite visual patterns were used on both the shallow and deep sides of the visual cliff. However, as the deep side pattern was

Reprinted by permission from *Psychonomic Science*, 1969, *14* (6), 251–255.

[1] This research was supported by grants from the National Science Foundation. I thank Mary Jane McGill and Richard Hodson for help in the main experiment and many others for help in the full range of data shown in Tables 1 and 2.

a moved closer to the glass (20 in., 10 in., rather than 40 in.), more and more infants could be coaxed to the mother, particularly infants less than 10 months of age, though even at 10-in. visual depth only 38 percent of the children crossed the glass to the mother (Walk, 1966). Could infants less than 10 months of age discriminate depth at these lesser depths? To answer this question, infants were called by the mother from

b the end of the center board or the bisection of shallow and deep sides, as in Fig. 1, rather than being coaxed across the deep side, as in Fig. 2. Under all conditions tested infants with the bisection condition chose the shallow side over 90 percent of the time. The question then arose: where will the overwhelm-

c ing choice of the shallow side break down, i.e., where is the threshold? Five inches of visual depth was chosen. Second, will the "younger" infants make "mistakes" with this new

d procedure? As an experimental control, an approximate equal density condition was included along with the regular one. Also, to compare with earlier experiments, infants were also coaxed across the deep side since so few infants were coaxed to the mother at 10-in. visual depth.

PROCEDURE

e The infant was placed on the wide end of the center board and called by the mother from the narrow end (Fig. 1) To reach the mother the infant was almost forced to leave the center board and crawl to her over the shallow or the deep side of the visual cliff. If he did not crawl to her within 3 min he was called by the mother from the shallow side. Normally, infants reached the mother as she stood at the narrow end of the center board. They were then replaced on the wide end of the center board and called by the mother from the deep side, then again replaced on the center board and called to her from the shallow side. The infant was next placed on the glass

f over the deep side and called by the mother from the shallow side; this was followed by placement on the shallow side with the mother calling him from the deep side. On the last trial he was again put on the wide end of the center board and called by the mother from the narrow end. The last trial was usually monocular, using an elastic

g eye patch with a small disposable gauze bandage beneath it. The only portion of the experiment reported here is the initial choice trial

Fig. 1 Mother calls to infant with
the bisection condition.

and the subsequent trial when the mother called from the deep side.

g The monocular data, combined with monocular data from other
experiments, has been reported elsewhere (Walk, 1968).

Apparatus.   The visual cliff was an enclosed box that measured
8 × 6 ft and was 40 in. high. The shallow side pattern, directly under
the glass, was either $\frac{3}{4}$-in. red and white checks (unequal density)

h or $\frac{1}{4}$-in. red and white checks (an approach toward equal density,
though actually with much coarser projected density from the deep
side). The $\frac{1}{4}$-in. pattern was also included as a comparison with
prior research. The deep side pattern was $\frac{3}{4}$-in. red and white checks

i 5 in. below the glass for the main part of the experiment, although
comparison is made with other experiments where the same pattern
was 10 in., 20 in., or 40 in. below the glass. On top of the glass a
center board bisected the glass into two equal segments. It was 14 in.
wide at one end and tapered to 3 in. wide at the other end. An 8-in.-
high border surrounded the apparatus to keep the infant from falling
off accidentally. Illumination was through cotton sheeting to diffuse
the light and minimize reflections. A Weston Master V light meter
that measured light directly reflected off of the patterns had a reading
of 1.3 ft-c on both shallow and deep sides. The apparatus is diagrammed in Walk (1966).

Subjects.   A total of 86 infants from $6\frac{1}{2}$ to 15 months of age were the
*S*s. The average age was 10.2 months (median 10.0 months), standard

j deviation 1.9 months. Fifty-two infants had the standard condition
($\frac{3}{4}$-in. shallow pattern) and 34 the other condition ($\frac{1}{4}$-in. shallow
pattern).

Table 1   Choice of Shallow or Deep Side for the Bisection Condition as a Function of Visual Depth
($\frac{3}{4}$-in. checked pattern on both shallow and deep sides)

VISUAL DEPTH	EFFECTIVE N	CHOICE OF		PER CENT SHALLOW
		SHALLOW	DEEP	
5 in.	41	30	11	73%
10 in.	28	26	2	93%
20 in.	32	32	0	100%
40 in.	22	21	1	95%

Note: Effective N only includes infants who crawled to mother and left board to either shallow or deep side.

RESULTS

Bisection Condition

As Table 1 shows, only 73 percent of the infants crawled to the shallow side with the 5-in. depth when the $\frac{3}{4}$-in. pattern was under the shallow side. Five inches thus represents an approximate threshold for differential visual depth perception for the human infant. The 5-in. condition, as compared to the other conditions listed on Table 1, is highly significantly different ($\chi^2 = 12.34$, p < .001); yet, the babies still choose the shallow side significantly more often than the deep side ($z = 2.81$, p < .01).[2] The $\frac{1}{4}$-in. pattern condition, surprisingly, gave 88 percent choice of the shallow side (21 shallow, 3 deep, 10 did not move from the center board of the 34 tested). However, the $\frac{1}{4}$-in. pattern condition did not give results significantly different from the regular condition so it is difficult to evaluate whether this has any significance.

The overall age differences were in the expected direction but far from statistically significant. The average age of the infants choosing the shallow side was 10.3 months, of those going to the deep side 9.8 months. A significant age difference

---

[2] "Chance" for the bisection condition must be, by definition, 50 percent since only infants that crawl to either shallow or deep side are represented. The coaxing condition has no way of assessing "chance" performance.

did appear when the eye patch was put on; then more young infants went to the deep side. This has been reported previously as part of the monocular study (Walk, 1968).

Coaxing Condition

While the overwhelming initial choice was toward the shallow side, most of the Ss were later coaxed across the deep side. With the regular $\frac{3}{4}$-in. pattern on the shallow side 82 percent of the Ss were coaxed across the deep side and 86 percent of the Ss went to the mother at the deep side with the $\frac{1}{4}$-in. shallow pattern. The most interesting aspect of these data is shown in Table 2 where comparable conditions, with only visual depth varied, are given. The $\frac{3}{4}$-in. pattern on the shallow side is held constant and visual depths of 0 in., 5 in., 10 in., 20 in., and 40 in. are represented. The age condition is particularly interesting here. At very definite depths (40 in.) infants older than 10 months of age and younger than that are similar: few cross to the mother. By 20 in. of visual depth more infants crawl to the mother at the deep side and the younger and older infants begin to diverge. The only significant difference, however, is at 10 in. of visual depth. Here 65 percent of the younger infants and only 21 percent of the older infants cross the deep side to the mother. By 5 in. of visual depth the two

k

Table 2 Infants Coaxed by Mother to the Deep Side as a Function of Visual Depth and Chronological Age
($\frac{3}{4}$-in. checks on both shallow and deep sides)

VISUAL DEPTH	N	NO GO	CRAWLED DEEP YOUNG	OLD	PER CENT YOUNG	OLD	P
40 in.	63	11	2	2	8%	7%	—
20 in.	63	11	8	6	32%	22%	—
10 in.	63	10	13	7	65%	21%	< .01
5 in.	50	6	12	24	92%	77%	—
0 in.	19	2	7	10	100%	83%	—

Note: "Young" is less than 10 months (300 days) of age; "old" is 10 months of age and more.

Fig. 2 Mother tries to coax infant across the deep side.

groups are almost similar again and the same for the 0-in. condition. Essentially, a threshold for motion sensitivity seems to have been crossed for the younger infants at 10 in. of visual depth and they begin to disregard visual cues and crawl to the mother. For the older infants this threshold is not reached until 5 in. of visual depth.

DISCUSSION

The most important finding of this experiment is its demonstration of multiple thresholds. The threshold for the bisection condition is at 5 in. of visual depth while the threshold for the coaxing condition is at 10-in. visual depth.

At 5 in. infants in the bisection condition begin to lose the overwhelming preference for the shallow side that was previously observed for visual depths of 10 in., 20 in., and 40 in. The preference drops from over 90 percent choice of the shallow side to 73 percent. Chronological age did not appear to be so important for the 5-in. bisection condition when infants were tested binocularly, but age was important for infants monocularized with an eye patch.

The 10-in. visual depth is sufficient for infants less than 10 months of age to be coaxed across the deep side. Older infants require about 5 in. of visual depth. The age difference must reflect the development of motion discrimination. This motion discrimination becomes precise enough so that older infants distinguish between the dangerous drop of 10 in. and the harmless 5-in. distance. Very precise discrimination is shown, precision not present until the infant is about 10 months of age.

We know from other research (Bower, 1966; Fantz, 1961) that human infants have some depth perception before they can crawl. The present studies confirm this by finding no age effects in the bisection condition when the visual depth is 10 in. or more. Here, infants of all ages almost unanimously crawl to the shallow side. The weakness shown near thresholds in the dynamic crawling situation of free locomotion fits in with observations of mothers who frequently report that their children crawl off places like beds and would injure themselves if unrestrained. The present experiment shows that such carelessness is partially based on a visual weakness and not entirely on such factors as poor locomotion or lack of foresight. By working near thresholds the researcher can discover the organismic factors (such as age, monocular vision) that interact with stimulus conditions during the development of depth perception.

REFERENCES

Bower, T. G. R. The visual world of infants. Scientific American, 1966, *215*, 80–92.

Fantz, R. L. The origin of form perception. Scientific American, 1961, 204, 66–72.

Walk, R. D. The development of depth perception in animals and human infants. Child Development Monograph, 1966, *31* (No. 107), 82–108.

Walk, R. D. Monocular compared to binocular depth perception in human infants. Science, 1968, *162*, 473–475.

Walk, R. D., & Gibson E. J. A comparative and analytical study of visual depth perception. Psychological Monographs: General & Applied, 1961, *75* (Whole No. 519).

CASE ANALYSIS

The question of "How do we know . . ." has long been a puzzle to thinking man. The philosophic school of thought called epistemology has mused over this question for centuries and it is not surprising to learn that the early psychologists tried to separate sensory impressions from cognitive processes. As psychology developed, the thinking of radical behaviorists taught that man was born without knowledge, that his mind at birth was a "blank slate" (*tabula rasa*), and that only through the sensory processes did man develop knowledge of his world. The modern period in psychology has modified this view. Sensory experiences and learning are still considered to play a major role in human existence but heredity also contributes to behavior. The controversy concerning the relative roles played by heredity and learning is often referred to as the nature—nurture issue and is one of the most challenging problems for the experimental psychologist.

Children seem to have an inborn aversion to sharp dropoffs. Although occasionally an unattended baby may fall off a bed, the general tendency of even young children is not to crawl off of a bed. This tendency appears at a very early age and without an opportunity to be learned. It has frequently been concluded, therefore, that some form of depth discrimination in humans and in a wide variety of other creatures seems to be innate. The development of the "visual cliff" by Walk and Gibson (1961) was an ingenious technique to test hypotheses of depth perception. In the original visual cliff experiment, mothers were asked to coax their children to the deep side of a device which contained a runway dividing a shallow side and a deep side. Of course, the "deep" side was an illusion created by placing a checkered pattern under a glass covering. Only 11 percent of the children would cross over the deep side while nearly all the children would go to their mothers on the shallow side. Could the aversion of a drop off be genetically encoded and only moderately affected by experience?

One basic reason the nature—nurture problem is difficult to investigate in the experimental laboratory is that the two factors are interrelated and inseparable. No organism has only heredity and no organism is completely devoid of experience. The best we can do is limit the influence of one factor and examine the other factors.

The present article by Walk was selected to illustrate the problem in experimentation with two inseparable factors, which in effect act as two independent variables. The specific behavior under study was the innateness of depth perception. This article is the most current of a series of articles in which a visual cliff serves as the principle apparatus.

This experiment is also presented in this series as it represents research in which the principal subject is an infant. Special care must be exercised with children as subjects. In addition to the capricious nature of infants which may have disconcerting effects on the data, very young children may experience distress in a new surrounding separate from their mothers. The author of the article on depth discrimination tried to reduce the latter possibility by having each infant's mother participate in the experiment.

In our series of articles we reviewed another article in which the perceptual processes were important ("Identification of cola beverages" by Thumin). The present experiment—in a very general sense—fits into the same category as the Thumin experiment, viz., perception. Thumin was concerned with taste while Walk is concerned with the ability of infants to discriminate depth when the depth is shallow.

Finally, this experiment may serve as a prototype for the development of scientific knowledge. The initial discovery that children can discriminate between a dropoff and a surface was reported by Walk and Gibson nearly ten years before this article appeared. Within that decade dozens of research papers have added a bit of information on depth perception in children as well as in rats, goats, hamsters, etc.; scientific development frequently inches along. The present experiment identifies another factor in infant visual perception.

REVIEW OF LITERATURE, STATEMENT OF PROBLEM, AND HYPOTHESIS

Section (a) is a brief review of the results obtained in other experiments. Of particular interest is the author's ability to succinctly state the basic findings so that no technical knowledge is needed. You should feel completely at ease with the statement of the problem in (b) after reading the introductory material. The problem of this study is essentially quantitative in nature, not qualitative, i.e., to investigate a level of depth discrimination, not to report the existence of visual discrimination.

This experiment has a clear dependent variable and several independent variables. Try to identify them and then develop a functional relationship, e.g.: "What behavior is a function of what condition?"

In (c) Walk uses the word "threshold" which means the least intensity of a stimulus (in this case, depth) which can be identified by the subject (in this case, infants). The second factor under experimental observation in this article is age which is mentioned in (d).

METHOD

Three topics are discussed in this section: procedure, apparatus, and subjects.

You will note that three different procedures were used: (e), (f), and (g). The first, (e), was used as a warm-up procedure; the second, (f), an experimental procedure; and the third, (g), a postexperimental procedure in which ancillary data is collected. These stages were not counterbalanced as the subsequent stage was acknowledged to be a function of its previous stage.

The apparatus or a modified version of it has been frequently utilized in visual cliff experiments within the last 10 years. Nevertheless, Walk gives enough information so the reader could, if he desired, replicate the apparatus. Note that the runway narrows from 14 inches to 3 inches. The effect of this narrowing is to force the child off the board either on the shallow or the deep side. Several different patterns were used (h). The shallow side had a checked pattern composed of $\frac{3}{4}$ inch or $\frac{1}{4}$ inch checks. The author was controlling for density which may have been a more significant factor than depth. Later on in this paragraph Walk measures the reflected light off of both surfaces and reports the ft-candle readings to be equal. He is concerned with measuring the effects of depth, not darkness or lightness. In case you missed the point (i), the deep side has a glass over it. Although infant research can be frustrating, it is not suggested that this frustration manifest itself in injury to subjects.

A brief description of the subjects appears in (j).

RESULTS

The author divides the results section into two categories: the bisectional condition and the coaxing condition. The overall results are presented in Tables 1 and 2 and in the text. If you read the article carefully, you will notice that Walk uses data gathered in other experiments for comparison purposes. This practice is not common and is usually done only when the procedure or apparatus is well standardized. The danger in using data from another study is that the sample may have changed, the apparatus may not be exactly the same as in the original experiment, the experimenter may have been replaced, etc. In the present experiment the author is justified in using previous data as this experiment is a continuation of a series of highly standardized procedures. Walk uses χ^2 (chi square) to interpret the data and reports that the preference for the shallow side is overwhelmingly greater than for the deep side.

The results of the coaxing condition are presented in (**k**). Walk offers statistical analysis for these data in terms of percentages (see Table 2) and P (probability of occurrence by chance). In (**l**) a statement of the results in terms of a threshold is made and briefly interpreted.

DISCUSSION

Walk embodies the fundamentals in his discussion section. First, he states what he believes to be the most important finding of the experiment (**m**). In the next two paragraphs he restates the results in a manner which is unencumbered by technical references and finally in the last paragraph he relates his results to other experiments. In (**n**) of the last paragraph the results of this study are applied to common observations of child behavior.

QUESTIONS

1. Take another nature–nurture issue (e.g., fear of fire) and design an experiment in which the influence of learning is minimized.

2. Take the data in Table 2 and draw a graph illustrating the relationship between depth, age, and percent who crawled deep.

3. Review the literature on the visual cliff in which infra-human sub-

jects are used. What are the advantages of these studies? The disadvantages?

4.   What is the purpose of using different sized squares? Would color be a factor with infants?

5.   Propose an alternate method of determining thresholds.

6.   Some personality theorists believe that adult personality traits have their origin in very young children. If this is true, offer an hypothesis regarding the personality of the subjects who were coaxed over the cliff. Would a follow-up study be worthwhile? What would you look for?

7.   What are the positive and perhaps the negative effects of using mothers as experimenters?

11

INTERFERENCE TRANSFER

INTERFERENCE TRANSFER PARADIGMS AND THE PERFORMANCE OF SCHIZOPHRENICS AND CONTROLS

Donald H. Kausler, *St. Louis University*
Charles V. Lair, *Veterans Administration Hospital, Knoxville, Iowa*
Roy Matsumoto, *University of Iowa*

A group of chronic schizophrenics (n = 18) and a group of control *S*s (hospital employees, n = 18) were contrasted on the A-C and A-Br negative transfer paradigms. As expected, both groups yielded negative transfer on both paradigms, with significantly greater negative transfer for A-Br relative to A-C in the schizophrenic group only (p < .001). As predicted from Mednick's associative interference hypothesis, the difference in negative transfer between paradigms was significantly greater in the schizophrenic group than in the control group (p < .05).[1]

a Mednick's (1958) formulation of learning theory and schizophrenia predicts a superiority of schizophrenics over normal control subjects for tasks with little <u>associative interference (that is, competing responses)</u> and a reversal with tasks involving high degrees of associative interference. Mednick and deVito (1958) reported validating evidence for this re-

Reprinted by permission from *Journal of Abnormal and Social Psychology*, 1964, *69* (5), 584–587. Published by American Psychological Association.
[1] This study was conducted while the first and third authors held summer appointments as research psychologist and summer student, respectively, for the Veterans Administration at the Veterans Administration Hospital, Knoxville, Iowa. Charles V. Lair is now at St. Louis University.

lationship when interference was manipulated via intralist cross-associates. However, in an extension of the Mednick and deVito study and with more adequate controls, Spence and Lair (1964) found no evidence to support the hypothesis that schizophrenics are more prone to associative interference than control subjects.

In both of the above studies associative interference was **b** manipulated extraexperimentally by means of word-association norms. It is conceivable that this technique is relatively insensitive to the hypothesized interaction between diagnostic category and associative interference and, perhaps, subject to **c** interactions with other variables, thus obscuring the effect of diagnostic category. An alternative approach is to rely upon **d** experimentally controlled manipulation of associative interference. Interference transfer paradigms offer this possibility. More specifically, the present study related diagnostic category (schizophrenic versus normal) to performance in the A-B, A-C and A-B, A-Br transfer paradigms.

The A-B, A-C paradigm is one in which the stimuli (A terms) of the first list (List 1) and the transfer list (List 2) are identical but the responses (B and C terms) differ. The A-B, A-Br paradigm is one in which the stimuli (A) and responses (B) are identical on the two lists but specific stimuli and responses are "re-paired," that is, new pairings occur, on List 2. A number of previous studies (e.g., Besch & Reynolds, 1958; Kausler **e** & Kanoti, 1963; Porter & Duncan, 1953; Twedt & Underwood, 1959) have reported greater negative transfer in the A-Br paradigm than in A-C, permitting the interference of greater amounts of associative interference in A-Br than in A-C. Generalizing from these studies on college subjects, negative transfer is to be expected for both paradigms in both of the present groups. However, from Mednick's hypothesis, it would be predicted that the difference in A-Br and A-C **f** transfer effects should be greater in schizophrenics than in normal controls.

METHOD

Subjects.   There were 18 male subjects in both the schizophrenic (Group S) and normal control (Group C) groups. The schizophrenics, with a mean age of 34.2 and a mean educational level of 11.6, were chronic patients (Veterans Administration Hospital, Knoxville, Iowa), all of whom were in partial remission, receiving tranquilizing drugs, and were without evidence of organic impairment or alcoholism. Group C consisted of male employees at the Veterans Administration Hospital, with mean age and mean educational level also 34.2 and 11.6, respectively.

Lists. A mixed list technique (Twedt & Underwood, 1959) was **g** used, with three transfer paradigms (A-C, A-Br, and C-D) being represented. The C-D pairs served as control pairs for evaluating A-C and A-Br effects relative to nonspecific sources (learning-to-learn, etc.) Lists 1 and 2 each contained nine pairs of unrelated words selected from the Minnesota word norms (Russell & Jenkins, 1954). List 2 was the same for all subjects and contained three pairs each for the three paradigms. Three variants of List 1 were employed (with one-third of each group assigned to each List 1) for control purposes and for greater generalization. The relationships of List 1 variants to List 2 followed the procedure of Twedt and Underwood (1959) and Kausler and Kanoti (1963). Three different serial orders were prepared for each list as a control for possible serial effects.

Procedure. Following instructions on the anticipation method and practice on a warm-up list of two pairs, each subject was given 15 trials on List 1 or practiced to a criterion of 1 perfect trial, whichever came first. Practice was limited to 15 trials in order to avoid a possible loss of cooperation in Group S and also to conform to the time availability in Group C. Practice on List 2 began approximately 2 minutes after completing List 1, with the intervening period being filled by informal conversation, and was continued for 10 trials or 1 perfect trial, whichever came first. A 4:4-second exposure rate and a 10-second intertrial interval were employed on both lists, with pairs being exposed by the anticipation method on a Lafayette drum. The 4:4-second rate was selected because of the anticipated difficulty of learning, particularly in Group S, with a faster pacing.

RESULTS AND DISCUSSION

Performance on Lists 1 and 2

On list 1, 13 out of 18 subjects in Group S and 15 out of 18 in Group C reached the criterion of 1 perfect trial. In terms of errors on List 1, the mean and standard deviation were 56.28 and 28.48, respectively, for Group S and 41.61 and 29.67 for Group C. On List 2, 8 out of 18 subjects in Group S and 15 out of 18 in Group C reached the criterion.[2] For List 2 errors, the mean and standard deviation were 37.49 and 19.54 for Group S and 16.83 and 12.14 for Group C.

Error scores on the two lists were analyzed by a 2×2 "mixed" analysis of variance, with diagnostic category (S and C) as the "between" variable and list (1 and 2) as the "within" variable. There was a significant effect for both diagnosis (between-diagnosis $MS = 5,618.00$, error $MS = 857.52$, $F = 6.55$, $df = 1/34$, $p < .025$) and lists (between-lists $MS = 8,536.89$, error $MS = 252.39$, $F = 34.82$, $p < .001$). However, the Diagnosis $\times$ List interaction did not approach significance ($F < 1$), suggesting that the groups differed in learning ability on List 1 as well as on List 2. Thus, the transfer results must be interpreted cautiously in that they probably reflect this difference in addition to whatever may be attributed to psychopathology.

A separate analysis was made for errors on each of the List 2 paradigms (C-D, A-C, and A-Br). For C-D pairs, mean errors were 8.22 and 3.44 for Groups S and C, respectively; for A-C pairs, comparable means were 12.44 and 6.39; and for A-Br pairs they were 16.83 and 7.00. A 2×2 mixed analysis of variance revealed significant main effects for both diagnosis (between-diagnosis MS 1,281.34, error $MS = 87.97$, $F = 14.57$, $df = 1/34$, $p < .001$) and paradigms (between-paradigm $MS = 336.58$, error $MS = 16.08$, $F = 20.93$, $df = 2/68$, $p < .001$).

h

---

[2] In terms of the specific paradigms on List 2, for Group S, the number of subjects reaching the criterion of one perfect trial (that is, three out of three pairs correct on a single trial) were 16, 12, and 10 on C-D, A-C, and A-Br pairs, respectively; for Group C, the corresponding frequencies were 17, 16, and 16.

h In addition, the Diagnosis × Paradigm interaction was significant ($MS = 62.19$, $F = 3.87$, $df = 2/68$, $p < .05$).

The interaction between diagnosis and paradigms offers some support for the hypothesis of greater associative interference in schizophrenics. That is, the difference in means between Groups S and C was greatest for A-Br pairs (11.83) and least for C-D pairs (4.78). However, for each paradigm the difference between Groups S and C was statistically significant (with t's = 2.28, 2.69, and 4.49, $df = 34$, for C-D, A-C, and A-Br, respectively). The difference on C-D pairs most likely reflects the differential learning ability noted above.

Transfer

Summary statistics are given in Table 1 for A-C and A-Br transfer as measured both absolutely (C-D errors—errors on the experimental paradigm) and relatively (absolute score/ C-D + experimental paradigm). As expected, both groups yielded negative transfer on both the A-C and A-Br paradigms. Table 1 also gives the results of t tests ($df = 17$) for the deviation of transfer from the null value of zero transfer. From this table, it may be noted that Group S yielded a highly significant negative transfer effect for A-Br as measured both absolutely and relatively and for A-C as measured absolutely. For relative A-C scores, the effect was of borderline significance. Similar findings were obtained for Group C, with the exception of relative scores on A-C where the effect fell considerably short of statistical significance.

In terms of differences between Groups S and C in the amount of transfer, the two groups differed significantly only in A-Br transfer as measured absolutely ($T = 2.85$, $p < .01$), with Group S displaying more negative transfer. All other comparisons yielded t's < 1.

As a test of the Mednick hypothesis per se, a difference score was computed for each subject by subtracting his absolute transfer score on A-C from that of A-Br. For Group S the mean difference was 4.39, which departs significantly from the null value of zero ($t = 4.10$, $df = 17$, $p < .001$). For Group C the mean difference was .62, which, although in the direction of greater negative transfer on A-Br than on A-C, did not

Table 1 Summary Statistics for A-C and A-Br Transfer and *t* Tests for Deviation from Zero Transfer

	ABSOLUTE TRANSFER PARADIGM						RELATIVE TRANSFER PARADIGM					
	A-C			A-Br			A-C			A-Br		
GROUP	M	SD	t	M	SD	t	M	SD	t	M	SD	t
S	−4.22	5.17	3.46***	−8.61	5.91	6.19***	−19.8	44.1	1.91*	−40.1	33.2	5.12***
C	−2.94	5.47	2.28**	−3.56	4.72	3.21***	−19.1	58.3	1.39	−29.3	48.2	2.58**

*p < .10.
**p < .05.
***p < .01.

approach statistical significance (t < 1). The difference between Groups S and C on these means was also significant
($t = 2.33$, $df = 34$, $p < .05$). Thus, associative interference was
more pronounced in the A-Br paradigm, relative to A-C, for
schizophrenics than for normal control subjects as predicted
from the Mednick hypothesis.

As noted in the Method section, several practical considerations necessitated a departure from the conventional
transfer procedure in which practice on List 1 is carried to
criterial performance. Since the modified List 1 procedure
employed in this study introduces a possible compounding
of error and trial measures, it was considered advisable to test
the associative-interference hypothesis on only those subjects
who had attained the criterion of one perfect trial on List 1
($n's = 13$ in Group S and 15 in Group C). These two subgroups
did not differ significantly in terms of trials to criterion with
means of 10.46 and 9.20 for schizophrenics and controls,
respectively; $t = 1.12$, $df = 26$, $p > .20$). For the schizophrenic
subjects the mean difference between A-Br and A-C transfer
scores was 5.08; the comparable value for control subjects was
$-.69$. The difference between these means was statistically
significant ($t = 2.38$, $df = 26$, $p < .05$), thus again supporting
the Mednick hypothesis of greater associative interference in
schizophrenics.

Finally, the results of this study indicate that the traditional
transfer paradigms offer sensitive analytical methods for investigating learning processes in schizophrenic and other
pathological groups. It should be noted that Lang and Luoto
(1962) have given a similar indication for mediational transfer
paradigms.

REFERENCES

Besch, Norma F., & Reynolds, W. F. Associative interference in
verbal paired-associate learning. *J. exp. Psychol.*, 1958, *55*,
554–558.
Kausler, D. H., & Kanoti, G. A. R-S learning and negative transfer
effects with a mixed list. *J. exp. Psychol.*, 1963, *65*, 201–205.
Lang, P. J., & Luoto, K. Mediation and associative facilitation in
neurotic, psychotic, and normal subjects. *J. abnorm. soc.
Psychol.*, 1962, *64*, 113–120.

Mednick, S. A. A learning theory approach to research in schizophrenia. *Psychol. Bull.*, 1958, *55*, 316–327.

Mednick, S. A., & de Vito, R. Associative response competition in
verbal learning of acute and chronic schizophrenics. Paper read
at the Eastern Psychological Association, Philadelphia, April
1958.

Porter, L. W., & Duncan, C. P. Negative transfer in verbal learning.
J. exp. Psychol., 1953, *46*, 61–64.

Russell, W. A., & Jenkins, J. J. The complete Minnesota norms
for responses to 100 words from the Kent-Rosanoff Word Association Test. Technical Report No. 11, 1954, University of
Minnesota, Contract N 8 onr 66216, Office of Naval Research.

Spence, Janet T., & Lair, C. V. Associative interference in the verbal
learning performance of schizophrenics and normals. *J. abnorm.
soc. Psychol.*, 1964, *68*, 204–209.

Twedt, Helen M., & Underwood, B. J. Mixed vs. unmixed lists in
transfer studies. *J. exp. Psychol.*, 1959, *58*, 111–116.

CASE ANALYSIS

Clinical psychologists have successfully identified certain differences between normal people and abnormal patients. These
observations have generally been restricted to the patient's
affective or emotional life. The present, well-controlled study is
an attempt to identify some specific differences in learning processes between a schizophrenic group and a control group.

For many years clinical psychologists have observed a tendency
for schizophrenic patients to exhibit imprecise verbal responses.
A further dimension of the patient's verbal problem may be his
tendency to use an inappropriate word or a neologism (new word).
A schizophrenic patient may seem remarkably normal for a short
period of time and then, for some unknown reason, will use a
word which is inappropriate to the conversation. For example,
one patient is reported to say "That was good farkle we had for
breakfast" and in the next instant say "I've got to farkle my hair"
or "I always keep my farkle in the bank." The word *farkle* may
have a unique meaning for the patient which is known only to
him. Psychologists have speculated about the cause of these
inappropriate responses with an aim to better understanding the

dynamics of schizophrenic behavior. One hypothesis regarding interfering responses is that previously learned responses are difficult for a patient to eradicate in a new learning situation. A term which describes this phenomenon is "associative interference." In the present study the authors experimentally induce associative interference and measure the relative effect of it on a schizophrenic group and a normal group.

The results present convincing evidence that the verbal processes of schizophrenics differed from normals. In addition, the authors of this well-designed and innovative study have successfully applied the techniques of the experimental learning laboratory to the study of a clinical problem. The findings reported in this paper not only have important theoretical implications but also provide psychologists with another technique for investigating pathological groups.

REVIEW

The hypotheses underlying this paper are derived from a theory developed by Mednick which predicts that schizophrenics will perform better than normals with simple tasks but poorer than normals with complex tasks involving competing responses. Kausler *et al.* suggest that one way to manipulate associative interference is to employ tasks which involve competing responses (**a**).

Ambigious findings have been reported regarding the hypothesis of associative interference and schizophrenics and part of that ambiguity may be traced to the nature of the task. Associative interference in previous studies was determined by having subjects learn new associates to presumably existing associates. Word-association norms (**b**) provided standardized data on the association initiated by the presentation of certain stimulus words (e.g., *man—women*; *table—chair*). An interference or competing task would pair *man* with *chair* and *table* with *women*. Subjects attempting to learn these new pairings would be likely to encounter a high degree of interference due to past learning. The method of using preexperimental associates may obscure the results as explained in (**c**). It is possible to experimentally control the associative interference (**d**), and the present authors suggest this method as a desirable alternative.

The next paragraph (**e**) is devoted to a thorough exposition of the learning and transfer models used in the study. Table 11.1 is an illustration of several transfer paradigms similar to those used in the Kausler experiment. The symbols "A" and "B" refer to stimulus and response, e.g., *apple* and *sand*. A subject would learn to respond by saying *sand* whenever the word *apple* appeared. Commonly, the words are presented by means of a memory drum, which is an apparatus containing a rotating drum on which individual verbal items are exposed to a subject. Following practice on an A–B (e.g., *apple–sand*) list, subjects receive a transfer model. In the present study the A–C (old stimulus–new response), A–Br (old stimulus–re-paired response), and C–D (new stimulus–new response) were used. Assume that words were employed, in the Br (re-paired) paradigm the original pairs were *apple–sand, eye–atom, sail–leg*; then the re-paired list could be *apple–leg, eye–sand*, and *sail–atom*. Kausler *et al*. point out that associative interference is high in the Br paradigm and it is easy to see that if you had learned to say *sand* when *apple* was presented and then were confronted with the confusing task of learning to say *leg* to *apple* and *sand* to *eye* that competing responses from the first learning task would probably retard the new learning.

Table 11.1

A–B		A–Br		A–C		C–D	
apple	sand	apple	leg	apple	jury	book	rabbit
eye	atom	eye	sand	eye	park	father	oil
sail	leg	sail	atom	sail	letter	eternal	bacon

The C–D model is a standard control paradigm used to evaluate the effect of "warm-up" or "learning to learn" during the first list and consists of new pairs.

Since associative interference is greater in the Br paradigm than in the A–C paradigm, the authors suggest that the difference between the performance on the tasks should be greater for schizophrenics than for normals (**f**).

METHOD

In this section a clear description of subjects, lists, and procedure is presented. Care was taken in this study to find a control group as similar to the schizophrenic group as possible. A form of matched groups were matched on sex (all males), age (mean age 34.2), and education (mean educational level 11.6).

Some recent studies on hospitalized psychiatric patients have used hospitalized nonpsychiatric patients as a control group. The rationale for using hospitalized patients as a control is that the experience of hospitalization may impede (or facilitate) certain intellectual functions which would have a direct influence on the dependent variable.

The mixed list technique (g) means that all paradigms (A–C, C–D, A–Br) were presented in a single nine-item list with three items designated A–C, three were C–D, and three were A–Br. Notice how many controls are used in this design. The words are unrelated, list two is identical for all subjects (the paradigmatic variations being made in the first list), three variants of list one were employed, and three orders of list presentation were used for each variation.

The procedure section gives sufficient detail to exactly replicate this study.

RESULTS

A brief statement concerning the original learning is made and then a more extensive analysis of the error scores is presented. The authors' conceptualized error score as an index of associative interference and as such it is a critical measure of the theory under investigation. The type of analysis of variance used was a "mixed" type with repeated measures made on one of the variables, i.e., the same subjects provided error data on list one and list two.

Errors within each paradigm (A–Br, A–C, and C–D) for schizophrenic and control groups were analyzed and that data is presented in (h). Since the relationship between A–C and A–Br errors of schizophrenic versus normals is a critical aspect of this study, we have illustrated it in Fig. 11.1.

The transfer data are given an exhaustive analysis with absolute

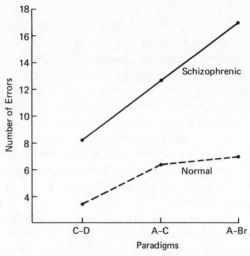

Fig. 11.1 Mean errors on second list for normals and schizophrenics.

and relative transfer reported in a table. In (i) a summary statement regarding the relative error production on the A–Br paradigm versus the A–C paradigm is made.

DISCUSSION

Some brief articles do not contain an identified discussion section but include a discussion under the heading of Results. The last paragraph succinctly states the findings and suggests future research.

QUESTIONS

1.   How could you apply the verbal learning technique described in this paper to psychodiagnosis?

2.   This research demonstrated differences in associative interference between a control and a schizophrenic group. Assume that psychotherapy is a relearning procedure. What learning reactions would you anticipate from a schizophrenic patient in psychotherapy based on the present results?

3.   Prepare a brief research proposal in which associative interference is measured with brain damaged patients.

4.   The schizophrenic patients in this study were receiving medication. Suggest techniques which evaluate the effect of tranquilizing drugs on learning performance.

5.   Within the context of Mednick's hypothesis, predict the results that may be found if the subjects are required to overlearn the first list.

6.   What was the purpose of the C–D group?

7.   Speculate as to whether associative interference is a function of age.

8.   Discuss the problem of finding a true control group for an abnormal group.

12

PAIN PERCEPTION

SELF-OBSERVATION AS A SOURCE OF PAIN PERCEPTION

Richard J. Bandler, Jr.
George R. Madaras, and
Daryl J. Bem
Carnegie-Mellon University

The hypothesis was tested that an individual's perception of a stimulus as uncomfortable or painful is partially an inference from his own observation of his response to that stimulus. Ss were required to observe themselves either escaping or enduring a series of electric shocks, all of the same physical intensity. As predicted, Ss rated the felt discomfort produced by the shocks to be greater in the "escape" condition than in the "no-escape" condition. Appropriate controls and auxiliary data helped to rule out alternative explanations of the obtained difference, and the record of Ss' galvanic skin responses suggested that actual physiological arousal was not serving as the basis for the Ss' discomfort ratings.[1]

An individual's perception of pain is only partially a function of the "pain producing" stimulus. This is apparent from

Reprinted by permission from *Journal of Personality and Social Psychology*, 1968, *9* (3), 205–209. Published by the American Psychological Association.

[1] This research was supported by National Science Foundation Grant GS 1452 awarded to the third author for the study of self-awareness and self-control. The authors are grateful to Jane Bandler for aiding in the data analysis and to Garlie Forehand and James Korn for critical comments on the manuscript.

the wide cultural differences in labeling stimuli as painful (e.g., childbirth; Melzack, 1961), from research on the long-familiar placebo effect (Beecher, 1959, 1960), and from the phenomenon of hypnotic analgesia (Barber, 1959, 1963) and **a** masochism (Brown, 1965). <u>On what basis, then, does an individual infer that a particular stimulus is painful?</u>

Recent research has indicated that the justification for enduring the aversive stimulation is one kind of information which may influence an individual's judgements of pain. Individuals who volunteered to participate in an experiment using painful electric shocks reported the shocks as less painful and were physiologically (GSR) less responsive than individuals who were forced to be in the experiment (Zimbardo, Cohen, Weinsenberg, Dworkin, & Firestone, 1966). Other research on emotional states has indicated that situational cues (in addition to actual physiological arousal) provide a second type of information which may influence an individual's judgements of bodily states, including pain and discomfort (Schachter & Singer, 1962). In fact, it has been shown that both the intensity of shock-produced pain and the willingness to tolerate such pain can be manipulated by supplying the individual with an alternative explanation for the physiological arousal he is experiencing (Nisbett & Schachter, 1966).

A recent analysis of self-perception by Bem (1965, 1966, 1967) suggests a third kind of information which may influence an individual's self-judgements of pain or discomfort. Bem's experimental work demonstrates that individuals use their own overt behavior as a basis for inferring their attitudes, their beliefs about external events, and the truthfulness of their own confessions. Self-perceptions, according to Bem, may thus be viewed as inferences that are functionally similar to the inferences an outside observer would draw from observing the individual's behavior. This suggests the possibility that an individual may actually use his own overt behavior in response to an aversive stimulus as evidence for deciding that the stimulus was, in fact, uncomfortable or painful. For example, an affirmative reply to the question, "Was that last electric shock uncomfortable?" may be functionally equivalent to the individual's (or an outside observer's) saying, "It must have b been; I (he) attempted to escape it as quickly as possible." In other words, an individual's behavioral response to an aversive stimulus, often treated as a dependent variable in pain research, may serve as an independent variable and partially control his perception of the stimulus as uncomfortable or painful.

c The present experiment explored this hypothesis by requiring the subject to observe himself either escaping or enduring a series of electric shocks, all of the same physical intensity. The subject was then asked to rate the amount of discomfort he experienced from each shock. It was hypothesized that the discomfort should be greater for the shocks from which the individual escaped than for shocks which he endured, since this is the inference that an outside observer of his behavior would draw. Appropriate controls were included in an attempt to rule out alternative explanations of any obtained difference between conditions. The subject's galvanic skin response (GSR) was also monitored to assess the possibility that actual physiological arousal serves as the basis for the subject's self-judgements of discomfort.

METHOD

Twelve male college students were hired for individual experimental sessions "to help us determine shock levels for future research." Upon arrival each subject was seated in a comfortable chair in a small acoustically tiled room. A small rectangular box with a Plexiglas covering faced the subject. Contained within the box were three 25-watt light bulbs (red, green, and yellow), which could be controlled by the experimenter from a separate room. A 7-point shock rating scale, which ranged from "not uncomfortable" to "very uncomfortable," was displayed on the wall in front of the subject. Each subject was told that the experiment involved electric shock and that the upper and lower limits of the scale would be determined prior to the start of the experiment by a pretest. The shock electrodes were taped to the subject's left hand and connected to a Lafayette Instrument Company inductorium. The GSR electrodes (zinc), of the

d Lykken type (Lykken, 1959), were attached to the subject's right hand. A zinc-sulfate electrode paste was used. GSR was monitored by a Fels dermohmeter and recorded on an Esterline-Angus recorder.

e After the subject's basal skin resistance was determined, a series of eight .5-second shocks, of varying physical intensities, was

e administered. The subject was asked to rate the discomfort produced by each shock in terms of the rating scale on the wall in front of him. A physical intensity of shock rated 6 in this pretest was used for all shocks during the ensuing experiment.

Following this pretest, the subject was instructed that there would be three different conditions during the experiment. He would feel a shock and .5 second later one of the three colored lights in the box in front of him would be illuminated, signaling the condition. The subject was told to hold the button on the left arm of the chair in his left hand. This button, at the experimenter's discretion, enabled the subject to terminate the shock. The subject was then told what to do in each of the three conditions.

Escape Condition.   This is the red condition [turned on red light]. In the red condition you will be able to turn off the shock by pressing the button in your left hand. In this condition, the red condition, you *should* press the button and turn off the shock. However, if the shock is not uncomfortable you may elect to not depress the button. The choice is up to you.

No Escape Condition.   This is the green condition [turned on green light]. In the green condition the button in your left hand will enable you to turn off the shock. In this condition, the green condition, you *should not* press the button and turn off the shock. However, if the shock is so uncomfortable that you feel you must turn it off, you may. Again, the choice is up to you.

Reaction-Time Condition.   This is the yellow condition [turned on yellow light]. The yellow condition is a reaction-time condition. We are interested in recording only the time that it takes you to press the button once the yellow light comes on. Therefore, please press the button as soon as the yellow light is illuminated. Your depression of the button *may* or *may not* turn off the shock.

Following each shock the subject was asked to rate the discomfort produced by each shock on the "shock rating scale." During the experiment each subject received 30 shocks of the physical intensity which he had rated 6 in the pretest.[2] If not terminated by the subject,

---

[2] Four shocks, all of a physical intensity rated 1 in the pretest, were also administered. These shocks serve to add credibility to the implication that different levels of shock were used during the experiment.

duration of shock was 2 seconds. To ensure in all conditions that each subject received a minimum of shock which could not be avoided, .5 second elapsed between the onset of shock and the onset of the light. The "escape" and "no escape" lights were reversed for half of the subjects; green for "escape" and red for "no escape," and the order of lights was randomized for each subject.

Thus, for the 10 shocks paired with the "escape" light, the subject pressed a button and terminated the shock. For the 10 shocks paired with the "no escape" light, the subject did not press the button which would have allowed him to terminate the shock. For the 10 shocks paired with the "reaction time" light, the subject pressed the button as soon as the light was illuminated. For five of these trials pressing the button terminated the shock. For the remaining five "reaction time" trials, pressing the button had no effect on the shock.

It will be noted that the subject's overt behavior is the same in this reaction-time condition as it is in the escape condition; he presses the button when the light is illuminated. But, the subject is not given the implied choice of pressing or not pressing the button in the reaction-time condition, and, as the instructions make clear, pressing the button does not necessarily terminate the shock. Thus, the button press should no longer be seen by the subject as a self-determined "escape" response and he should not infer his discomfort from it. Discomfort ratings should therefore be significantly higher in the escape condition than in the reaction-time condition.

DEMAND CONTROL CONDITION

It is conceivable that the predicted differences between conditions could arise in the present experiment as an artifact. That is, subjects may be led to entertain hypotheses about the purpose of the experiment which would lead them to anticipate more severe shocks in the escape condition than in the other conditions, thus producing a "demand characteristic" artifact of the type discussed by Orne (1962). To check on this possibility, an additional 10 subjects were employed who were treated the same as the experimental subjects except that they were not required to experience the 30 constant shocks. Instead, following the pretest and the instructions for the three conditions, they were asked to fill out a questionnaire about their anticipations concerning the experiment. The crucial questions were:

I expect to receive the following levels of shock during the course of the experiment (circle each expected level):

a. in the Red condition   1 2 3 4 5 6 7
b. in the Green condition   1 2 3 4 5 6 7
c. in the Yellow condition   1 2 3 4 5 6 7

During the course of the experiment I expect the average shock in the Red condition to be (circle answer):

greater than
equal to
less than

the average shock in the Green condition.

A final question asked the subject to explain his answer to the latter item.

The total experiment, then, assesses the hypothesis that an individual's observation of his own behavior can serve as a source of evidence for his perception of pain or discomfort. The hypothesis predicts that discomfort ratings in the escape condition should be greater than those in the no escape and reaction-time conditions.

RESULTS AND DISCUSSION

The experimental test of the hypothesis required the successful manipulation of the subjects' escape and no escape behavior. Accordingly, two of the subjects were excluded from the analysis since they escaped on all trials in both the escape and no escape conditions. The remaining 10 subjects escaped on 96 percent of the escape trials and did not escape on 85 percent of the no escape trials. Removal of the few incorrect trials does not alter the conclusions reached, and the analysis reported here includes them, providing a conservative test of the hypothesis.

The main prediction is that the ratings of discomfort produced by the shock in the escape condition will be greater than those in the no escape condition. It is seen in the first column of Table 1 that the mean ratings of discomfort in the escape condition are significantly higher than those in the no escape condition ($p < .01$, two tailed).

Table 1 further reveals that the button press must be seen as a self-determined "escape" response if it is to serve as the basis of inference for the individual's discomfort judgement. The reaction-time condition, which required the subject to push

Table 1 Mean Shock-Discomfort Ratings and Comparisons of Direction of Ratings for the Experimental Group

CONDITION	M RATING[b]	DIRECTION OF M RATING	NO. S	DIRECTION OF M RATING	NO. S
Escape (A)	5.14	Escape > No escape	8	Escape > Reaction time	8
No escape (B)	4.72	Escape = No escape	1	Escape = Reaction time	0
Reaction time (C)	4.66	Escape < No escape	1	Escape < Reaction time	2
	t		p		p
A vs. B	3.88**	Exact probability[a]	.01	Exact probability	.01
A vs. C	2.40*				
B vs. C	0.30				

[a]Exact probability is defined as the probability of a distribution "at least as deviant as" the one considered.
[b]$n = 10$.
*$p < .05$, two-tailed.
**$p < .01$, two-tailed.

the button but did not permit him to interpret his response as a self-determined escape response, yields discomfort ratings significantly lower than those in the escape condition ($p < .05$, two tailed) and not significantly different from those found in the no escape condition.

Columns 2 and 3 reveal the consistency of the predicted effects: 8 of the 10 subjects rated "escape" shocks as more uncomfortable than either "no escape" or "reaction time" shocks. The exact probability of this distribution is less than .01 by a Chapanis (1962) multinomial significance test.

j   Although these results are consistent with our conceptual analysis, it is necessary to examine a number of alternative explanations that might account for the obtained difference.

First, because the subject terminated all shocks in the escape condition, these shocks were necessarily of a shorter duration than those in the other conditions. It might be the case, then, that discomfort was simply a function of shock duration, with shorter shocks being perceived as more severe. This explanation is somewhat implausible, and is not supported by our other data. In the reaction time condition, the five non-terminated shocks were rated slightly more uncomfortable than the five terminated shocks (4.80 versus 4.52, $t = 2.14$). Shock duration would thus not seem to be able to account for the obtained differences between experimental conditions.

k

Second, a "demand characteristic" artifact may account for the observed rating difference. For some reason the subjects may have hypothesized that the experimenter would administer more intense shocks on those trials on which they were urged to escape. This possibility was checked, it will be recalled, by running a separate demand control condition, in which 10 additional subjects were asked to fill out a questionnaire about their anticipations concerning the experiment. In one question subjects were asked to circle the levels of shock expected in each condition. If a "demand" type of artifact were to account for the observed rating difference, it would be expected that the mean of the levels of shock circled in the escape condition would be greater than the mean of the levels circled in the other conditions. In fact, as seen in the first column of Table 2, the means show an insignificant reversal. In addition, when asked to circle whether the expected average

l

Table 2 Mean Shock-Discomfort Ratings and Comparison of Direction of Ratings for the Demand Control Group

CONDITION	M RATING[a]	DIRECTION OF M RATING	NO. S	DIRECTION OF M RATING	NO. S
Escape (A)	3.93	Escape > No escape	4	Escape > Reaction time	4
No escape (B)	4.38	Escape = No escape	3	Escape = Reaction time	4
Reaction time (C)	4.10	Escape < No escape	3	Escape < Reaction time	2
	t		p		p
A vs. B	−0.82	Exact probability	.74	Exact probability	.53
A vs. C	−0.47				
B vs. C	0.85				

[a]N = 10.

l level of shock in the escape condition was to be greater than, equal to, or less than the expected average level of shock in the no escape or reaction time condition; 6 of the 10 subjects reported the expected average shock in these two conditions to be equal to, or greater than, the expected average shock in the escape condition (Columns 2 and 3 of Table 2). Clearly, these results do not differ from chance expectation. Thus, these subjects' expectations would appear to run counter to the experimental hypothesis as often as they would confirm it artifactually. A "demand characteristic" artifact, then, does not appear to offer an alternative explanation of the results.

Finally, the research of Schachter and Singer (1962), Nisbett and Schachter (1966), and Valins (1967) suggests that subjects might use actual physiological arousal as a basis for self-judgements of discomfort. That is, if the subjects were more aroused in the escape condition than in the other conditions they might have rated the shocks as more painful for that reason. To assess this possibility subjects' GSR was monitored.[3] GSR was defined as a change in resistance occurring 1–4 seconds following shock onset. The mean GSR converted

m to change in log conductance $\times$ 1000 (Montagu & Coles, 1966) for the escape condition is 28.88; for the no escape condition it is 29.78; and for the reaction-time condition, 33.27. None of these differences is significant, and, further, the ordering of subjects' ratings of discomfort is the exact reverse of these. There is no evidence, then, that the subjects' ratings of discomfort were dependent on any internal cues that covary with changes in GSR. We conclude, then, that the obtained rating differences can be attributed to subjects' inferences

n from observation of their own response to the electric shock.

It may be that hypnotic analgesia and placebo "pain-relief" reflect the operation of the same process illustrated in this experiment. That is, through hypnosis or placebo suggestion the individual is led to suppress an avoidance or escape response to the aversive stimulus, and his perception of pain or discomfort is in turn predicated upon his observation of that

[3] GSR data for one of the subjects could not be obtained owing to equipment failure.

response inhibition. Thus, in contrast with the usual interpretation of such phenomena, which argues that the perception of pain is directly affected by the suggestion, the present interpretation views the suggestion as merely a way of altering the individual's overt behavior, with the perception following as a self-judgement from his observation of that behavior.

REFERENCES

Barber, T. X. Toward a theory of pain: Relief of chronic pain by prefrontal leucotomy, opiates, placebos, and hypnosis. *Psychological Bulletin*, 1959, *59*, 430–460.

Barber, T. X. The effects of hypnosis on pain. *Psychosomatic Medicine*, 1963, *25*, 303–333.

Beecher, H. K. *Measurement of subjective responses: Quantitative effects of drugs.* New York: Oxford University Press, 1959.

Beecher, H. K. Increased stress and effectiveness of placebos and "active" drugs. *Science*, 1960, *132*, 91–92.

Bem, D. J. An experimental analysis of self-persuasion. *Journal of Experimental Social Psychology*, 1965, *1*, 199–218.

Bem, D. J. Inducing belief in false confessions. *Journal of Personality and Social Psychology*, 1966, *3*, 707–710.

Bem, D. J. Self-perception: An alternative interpretation of cognitive dissonance phenomena. *Psychological Review*, 1967, *74*, 183–200.

Brown, J. S. A behavioral analysis of masochism. *Journal of Experimental Research in Personality*, 1965, *5*, 65–70.

Chapanis, A. An exact multinomial one-sample test of significance. *Psychological Bulletin*, 1962, *59*, 306–310.

Lykken, D. T. Properties of electrodes used in electrodermal measurement. *Journal of Comparative and Physiological Psychology*, 1959, *52*, 629–634.

Melzack, R. The perception of pain. *Scientific American*, 1961, *204*, 41–49.

Montagu, J. D., & Coles, E. M. Mechanism and measurement of the galvanic skin response. *Psychological Bulletin*, 1966, *65*, 261–279.

Nisbett, R. F., & Schachter, S. Cognitive manipulation of pain. *Journal of Experimental Social Psychology*, 1966, *2*, 227–236.

Orne, M. T. On the social psychology of the psychological experiment: With particular reference to demand characteristics and their implications. *American Psychologist*, 1962, *17*, 776–783.

Schachter, S., & Singer, J. Cognitive, social, and physiological determinants of emotional state. *Psychological Review*, 1962, *69*, 379–399.

Valins, S. Cognitive effects of false heart-rate feedback. *Journal of Personality and Social Psychology*, 1967, *4*, 400–408.

Zimbardo, P. G., Cohen, A. R., Weisenberg, M., Dworkin, L., & Firestone, I. Control of pain motivation by cognitive dissonance. *Science*, 1966, *151*, 217–219.

CASE ANALYSIS

The existence of wide variations in the apparent "painfulness" of stimuli between individuals within the same culture and between different cultures suggests that pain perception is based not only upon the "painful" stimulus, but upon a variety of personal and social factors. For example, in previous studies it has been shown that a subject's tolerance for pain and his judgements of the painfulness of an electric shock may vary depending upon whether or not he is undergoing the shock voluntarily. Still another factor which appears to influence a subject's judgements of painfulness may be his own observations as to how he behaves in response to the painful stimulus. Thus watching himself jump away may lead him to report that the shock was very painful, while if (for whatever reason) he bears it without flinching, he may report it as being relatively less painful.

The present experiment is therefore not merely concerned with pain perception but with the larger problem of how—on the basis of observations of his own behavior—an individual may gradually come to develop a set of perceptions about his own attitudes, beliefs, or feelings.

In addition to the theoretical issues raised above, this article is interesting from a methodological standpoint. You should notice the measurement techniques employed in this experiment. The authors were well aware of the wide range of human reactions to electrical stimuli and tried to control for possible individual differences. Another feature of this article is the demand control condition. The authors speculate that the results could have been caused by an artifact, or a result not caused by the variable under investigation but by some uncontrolled and perhaps unknown factor. They check this possibility by examining 10 more subjects on an alternate task. In Chapter 5 we reviewed the importance of adequate experimental control. One special type of control is necessary when a "demand characteristic" artifact may exist. Demand characteristic artifacts are particularly problematic in social and clinical research. The essence of this variable is that subjects and sometimes experimenters react not to the objective experimental condition, but to a role they think they should be playing. For example, a newly institutionalized psychiatric patient may behave psychotically because he is fulfilling a role others expect of him rather than because of any deep psychological problem. In the present study the authors anticipated that their subjects may have formed a hypothesis about the nature of the experiment which would affect the results. In an attempt to measure the influence of the suspected "demand characteristic" an additional control group was asked to fill out a questionnaire about their anticipation regarding the experiment. Finally after the results are analyzed the authors reflect on their findings in an extensive discussion section.

REVIEW

The perception of pain is determined by numerous factors in addition to the stimulus alone. The authors quickly review some of the basic antecedents to pain perception in the first paragraph and then state the problem of this experiment in the form of a question (a).

The following two paragraphs review three theories as to the type of information which influences pain perception. They are (1) forcing subjects into a painful situation, (2) situational cues which may influence pain perception, and (3) self-perception as evidence for pain. The last sentence in the third paragraph (b) states the hypothesis to be tested in this study. In (c) a brief statement of the experimental technique is presented to make the transition to the method section more comprehensible.

METHOD

This method section requires careful reading because of its complexity. The authors have organized this section by describing the subjects (12 male students), the physical setting, the instructions, the task, and the apparatus. Try to picture the physical setting as described by the authors. A box with three colored bulbs and a 7-point scale which ranged from very uncomfortable to very comfortable are placed before each subject.

A reference is made to GSR recordings. The initials stands for Galvanic Skin Response which is a measure of skin conductance. Under different emotional conditions the GSR may change drastically but imperceptibly to the subject. The GSR apparatus enables the experimenter to measure moment-to-moment variations in skin resistance. "Lie detectors" employ a GSR measure as one index of emotion.

In previous reviews we have admonished the beginning researcher to include only pertinent facts in his article. In (d) you may think that Bandler, Madaras, and Bem have presented too many details; they even identify the chemical composition of the paste which was placed between the subject's hand and the galvanic skin response recording instrument. However, the experimenters realized that several types of GSR paste are commonly used and that GSR is partly a function of the conductivity of the paste.

In (e) the shock level judged one unit down from "very uncomfortable" was determined for each subject. Since pain perception and the interpretation of "very uncomfortable" varies widely between subjects, this early standardization was necessary.

Section (f) presents a practical demonstration of counterbalancing and randomization as discussed in Chapter 5. The color of the lights used for the escape and no escape treatments were counterbalanced so that for half of the subjects the red light signalled the "escape" condition and for half of the subjects the red light signalled the "no escape" condition. The authors could have achieved a more complete counterbalancing if there had been a condition in which the red light signalled the "reaction time condition. The order of presentation of lights (or the order of experimental conditions) was randomized for each subject. This eliminates the various problems of order effects occurring for within-subject designs discussed in Chapter 5.

Three conditions, each contingent on the color of the bulb lighted, are described: Escape Condition, No Escape Condition, and Reaction-Time Condition. Read each of these conditions carefully. The Demand Control Condition is an extremely important control (**g**) and was included to measure the effect of the instructions on anticipated pain perception. "Demand characteristics" is a persistent methodological problem with research on humans. In an experimental situation the subject may not be responding to the independent variable as such but may be responding in a manner that he feels is appropriate in the situation, or in a way that he feels the experimenter wants him to respond, or in some manner based on his assumptions about what the experiment is all about. Thus the subject's response is not only to the independent variable but also to the demand characteristics of the total experimental situation. This presents an undesirable extraneous variable in interpreting the results and the authors instituted a control condition to illuminate this as a possible interpretation for their results.

In case you missed the hypothesis, or forgot it after reading through the method section, it is repeated in (**h**).

RESULTS

Experimentation with human subjects is always fascinating. One can only speculate as to the reaction of the two subjects who were excused (**i**). Of the remaining subjects a greater pain to the shocks in the escape condition was reported than in the no escape condition.

Bandler *et al.* effectively use tables to present part of the data generated by this research. The statistical analysis used was a two-tailed *t* test which is used to identify differences between means. A two-tailed test is one in which the hypothesis does not specify the direction of the expected results.

DISCUSSION

A separate discussion section is not identified in this article. However, at (**j**) the discussion begins.

Three alternate explanations of the results are considered and each rejected on the basis of logical analysis and/or empirical evidence. These concepts are reviewed and presented in paragraphs (**k**), (**l**), and (**m**).

In (**n**) the researchers plainly state their conclusion. The final paragraph is a reflection on the results. It has real value as the distinction between suggestion as a cause of pain perception and suggestion as a way of changing the subject's overt behavior is made.

THE ETHICS OF RESEARCH

The use of electric shock in this experiment leads into the question of the ethics of psychological research. In the Ethical Standards Casebook (1967) guidelines are set down for the handling and treatment of human and animal subjects. Essentially, the guidelines state that it is unethical for a researcher to treat the subject in a manner that may be psychologically or physically harmful to him. However, these guidelines do not spell out exactly what is ethical or unethical in every specific situation and the experimenter must use his own judgement in any given situation. Perhaps the most noticeable variance in the standards deals with the treatment of humans versus animal subjects. There are many things that researchers can do with animals (e.g., administer brain lesions) that would not be done with humans. While the subject of research ethics is too vast to discuss here, it should be noted that if the experimenter has any reason to believe that an experimental treatment might be harmful either psychologically or physically to a human subject, he should refrain from using this treatment. Further, if the researcher has reason to believe that the experimental treatment may cause the subject a considerable amount of discomfort, it is best to inform the subject of the nature of the discomfort prior to his volunteering for the experiment. Bandler *et al.* informed the subjects that the experiment involved shock and they had a choice as to whether or not they wanted to participate in it.

QUESTIONS

1.   Review the importance of the reaction-time condition. What relevance did this have for the discussion section?

2.   The experimenters counterbalanced the lights for the "escape condition" and for the "no escape condition." Discuss the possible cultural effect on pain perception as a function of colors.

3.   Why was a high shock level, as initially felt, used for testing? What results may have been obtained for lower voltage?

4.   For a major project, select one of the three alternate hypotheses and design a direct test of it.

5.   Describe several practical and creative ways you could use the results of this study.

6.   Behavioral therapies sometimes emphasize desensitization as a part of the therapeutic process. Is there a conflict between this study and therapeutic desensitization? Support your speculation with empirical results.

7.   What other physiological measures might have been observed to measure pain perception?

8.   Would self-observation as a source of pain perception interact with anxiety?

13

INFORMATION PROCESSING

INFORMATION PROCESSING IN
CHILDREN AS A FUNCTION
OF ADULT MODEL, STIMULUS
DISPLAY, SCHOOL GRADE,
AND SEX

Patrick R. Laughlin
Irene L. Moss, and
Susan M. Miller
Loyola University, Chicago

In order to study the influence of the information-processing strategy of an adult model on the subsequent strategy of children, 216 Ss solved modified twenty-questions problems. A $3 \times 2 \times 3 \times 2 \times 2$ repeated-measures factorial design was used with the following variables: (a) information processing of model (hypothesis scanning, constraint seeking, or control), (b) stimulus display (pictorial or verbal), (c) school grade (three, five, or seven), (d) sex (male or female), (e) problems (two per S). Major results were: (a) fewer questions to solution with the constraint-seeking model than the hypothesis-testing model or control, which did not differ, (b) both a higher percentage of constraints and higher average number of items included per question with the constraint-seeking model than the control or hypothesis-testing model, and with the control than the hypothesis-testing model, (c) both a higher percentage of constraints and higher number of items per question for seventh than fifth and third graders, and for fifth than third graders, (d) significant Model × Grade interactions for both percentage of constraints and items per

Reprinted by permission from *Journal of Educational Psychology*, 1969, 60 (3), 188–193. Published by the American Psychological Association.

question, (e) no effects for stimulus display, sex, or successive problems on any measure.[1]

Bruner, Olver, and Greenfield (1966) assume that the organization of a child's cognitive processes will be reflected in the questions he asks, and that the study of question asking is thus a method of externalizing the child's internal thought processes. In one of their experiments grade-school children played a modified game of "twenty questions" with E. The E selected one object from an array of 42 drawings of common objects (e.g., a cow, sailboat, boy) and the child attempted to determine what object E had in mind by asking questions that could be answered by a "yes" or "no."

In this situation the authors distinguished two basic types of strategies or problem-solving methods used by the children: (a) hypothesis scanning, (b) constraint seeking. In hypothesis scanning the child asked a series of unrelated specific questions, for example, "Is it the cow?" or "Is it the sailboat?" For a child who used the strategy of hypothesis scanning the number of questions necessary to solve the problem was determined purely by chance, and no underlying information processing was demonstrated beyond the simple ability to formulate specific questions. In constraint seeking the child asked a question comprehensive enough to include at least two objects, for example, "Is it red?" or "Is it larger than a dog?" and hence gained information from either a "yes" or "no" answer to his question. The strategy thus required an ability to perceive and categorize the objects in terms of subordination and superordination. In general, the use of constraint seeking relative to hypothesis scanning increased with age, and corresponded to a change from perceptual to functional, and from complexive to superordinate, bases of equivalence.

In a theoretical explanation of childrens' learning, Bandura and Walters (1963; Bandura, 1965; Walters & Parke, 1964)

[1] Supported by the United States Office of Education, Small Projects Program, Grant No. 7–E–103. The authors wish to express their appreciation to José A. Aguerre, William J. Lotak, and Sandra J. Polk for assistance in the collection and analysis of the data. Susan M. Miller is now at Ohio University.

have formulated a developmental theory in which the major concept is learning by imitation. Rather than the complicated **c** process of successive approximations and reinforcement postulated by most learning theories, the child learns by imitating the behavior of his formal and informal models. Thus, the purpose of the following experiment was to relate the approaches of Bruner *et al.* (1966) and Bandura and Walters **d** (1963) in a study of the information-processing behavior of children who had previously observed an adult model solve the problems by using a strategy of hypothesis scanning or constraint seeking. In control conditions the adult model simply posed the problem to the child, but did not first solve a problem himself. Two types of stimulus displays were used, pictorial displays such as those of Bruner *et al.*, and verbal displays, in which words replaced the corresponding drawings (e.g., the word "cow" replaced the drawing of a cow). The *S*s were equal numbers of boys and girls in Grades 3, 5, and 7.

METHOD

Design and Subjects.   The experimental design was a 3 × 2 × 3 × 2 × 2 repeated-measures factorial with the following variables: (*a*) information processing of model (hypothesis scanning, constraint seeking, or control), (*b*) stimulus display (pictorial or verbal), (*c*) school grade (three, five, or seven), (*d*) sex (male or female), (*e*) problems (two for each *S*). The *S*s were 216 children from four Chicago parochial grade schools. Six *S*s were randomly assigned to each of the 36 experimental treatments.

Information Displays.   The pictorial display was the same as used by Bruner *et al.* (1966), consisting of 42 drawings of common objects in a 6 × 7 matrix. The verbal display consisted of the lettered names of the same objects in the same arrangement. A smaller sample **e** pictorial or verbal array consisting of 16 objects in a 4 × 4 matrix was used to demonstrate the problem during the initial instructions. *Procedure and Instructions.*   In all conditions *E* instructed *S* as follows:

Here is a board with 16 drawings (words). And here is a box with 16 pieces of paper, one for each of the drawings (words). First we will take one of the slips of paper, and then ask questions to decide which drawing (word) is on the piece of paper. You can ask any questions at all that I can answer by saying "yes" or "no." And you can have as many questions as you need, but try to find out the right answer in as few questions as you can. All right? Now take a piece of paper from the box, but don't look at it.

In hypothesis-scanning and constraint-seeking conditions E continued:

First I am going to ask the questions to decide which drawing (word) is on the piece of paper. I'm going to show you one way to find out the answer, but you must remember that it is not the only way.

In hypothesis-scanning conditions E then asked a predetermined and memorized random series of specific hypotheses (e.g., "Is it the dog?") until he solved the problem. Under constraint-seeking conditions he solved the problems as efficiently as possible by a series of constraints beginning from the standard constraint "Is it an animal?" After observing E solve the problem, S then solved two problems selected by drawing pieces of paper from a new set of 42 pieces corresponding to the pictorial or verbal array. In control conditions S solved one problem from the sample 4 × 4 array and two from the full array. In all conditions the problem was solved when S asked the correct hypothesis. Four Es (two male and two female) each ran a proportionate number of Ss in all 36 conditions.

RESULTS

Means for the 36 treatment groups for number of questions to solution, percentage of constraints, and average number of items included per question, for totals over the two problems on the full stimulus display, are given in Table 1. Results of analyses of variance on the three measures are given in Table 2. Since none of the main effects of successive problems or any of its interactions with other variables were significant, both Table 1 and Table 2 are for totals over the two problems only, omitting means and analyses of variance for successive problems.

Number of Questions to Solution

The effect of the model was significant, $F = 3.30, df = 2/180$, $p < .05$. By Duncan multiple-range comparisons the constraint-seeking model resulted in fewer questions to solution than the control ($p < .01$) or hypothesis-scanning ($p < .001$) model, while the control and hypothesis-scanning models did not differ. No other main effects or first-order interactions were significant.

Percentage of Constraints

Each question was scored as either a specific hypothesis or a constraint. The question was scored as a specific hypothesis if it referred to only one object (e.g., "Is it the cow?"), and as a constraint if it referred to at least two objects (e.g., "Is it an animal?"). Thus, by definition a constraint could not be the final solution to the problem. "Pseudoconstraints" (Bruner *et al.*, 1966), or questions phrased like a constraint but actually referring to only one object (e.g., "Does it have a sail?" when only one of the objects had a sail) were also scored, but their number was extremely small in all conditions, and hence they were not further analyzed. The number of constraint questions was then divided by the total number of questions on the problem to obtain the percentage of constraints. The effect of the model was significant, $F = 30.13$, $df = 2/180$, $p < .001$. By Duncan comparisons there was a higher percentage of constraints with the constraint-seeking model than the control ($p < .001$) or the hypothesis-scanning ($p < .001$) model, and more for the control than the hypothesis-scanning model ($p < .001$). The effect of grade was significant, $F = 13.04$, $df = 2/180$, $p < .001$. Seventh graders had a higher percentage of constraints than fifth ($p < .01$) or third ($p < .001$) graders, and fifth more than third ($p < .001$).

The Model × Grade interaction was significant, $F = 2.50$, $df = 4/180$, $p < .05$, and is presented in Fig. 1. This interaction was further analyzed in two ways by Duncan comparisons: (*a*) hypothesis-scanning versus constraint-seeking versus control within each grade level, (*b*) Grades 3 versus 5 versus 7

Table 1   Mean Number of Questions to Solution, Percentage of Constraints, and Average Number of Items Included per Question, for Totals over Two Problems

DISPLAY	NUMBER OF QUESTIONS	PERCENTAGE OF CONSTRAINTS	ITEMS PER QUESTION
	HYPOTHESIS SCANNING		
Pictorial			
Grade 3			
Male	32.8	.20	2.60
Female	16.3	.16	4.46
Grade 5			
Male	26.8	.08	2.46
Female	34.5	.11	4.02
Grade 7			
Male	28.8	.83	9.39
Female	36.8	.32	5.32
Verbal			
Grade 3			
Male	60.7	.20	2.78
Female	36.7	.19	2.83
Grade 5			
Male	43.2	.11	2.77
Female	24.5	.46	4.13
Grade 7			
Male	40.3	.24	3.27
Female	45.0	.21	3.99
	CONSTRAINT SEEKING		
Pictorial			
Grade 3			
Male	44.8	.61	5.44
Female	43.0	.23	3.23
Grade 5			
Male	24.8	1.17	8.68
Female	24.2	1.03	9.33
Grade 7			
Male	27.7	1.04	6.58
Female	17.7	.96	7.57

Note.—Maximum percentage of constraints is 2.00.

Table 1   (continued)

DISPLAY	NUMBER OF QUESTIONS	PERCENTAGE OF CONSTRAINTS	ITEMS PER QUESTION
CONSTRAINT SEEKING			
Verbal			
Grade 3			
Male	32.3	.36	3.32
Female	31.7	.69	5.55
Grade 5			
Male	24.7	1.06	8.90
Female	34.0	.87	7.11
Grade 7			
Male	19.5	1.14	7.20
Female	26.7	1.08	7.52
CONTROL			
Pictorial			
Grade 3			
Male	36.5	.33	3.53
Female	31.2	.41	3.76
Grade 5			
Male	42.2	.61	7.17
Female	30.7	.20	2.72
Grade 7			
Male	42.5	.54	4.89
Female	39.7	.64	5.80
Verbal			
Grade 3			
Male	49.0	.45	5.82
Female	40.0	.19	3.30
Grade 5			
Male	21.2	.71	5.51
Female	30.8	.41	4.01
Grade 7			
Male	31.8	.90	7.85
Female	27.5	.79	7.57

within each model level. For the third graders there was a higher percentage with the constraint-seeking model than the hypothesis-scanning model ($p < .01$), while neither the constraint-seeking nor hypothesis-scanning models differed

Table 2 Analyses of Variance for Number of Questions to Solution, Percentage of Constraints, and Average Number of Items Included per Constraint, for Totals over Two Problems

SOURCE	DF	NUMBER OF QUESTIONS		PERCENTAGE OF CONSTRAINTS		ITEMS PER CONSTRAINT	
		MS	F	MS	F	MS	F
Model (M)	2	596	3.30*	3.20	30.13**	64.3	9.59**
Display (D)	1	36	<1	.03	<1	.8	<1
Grade (G)	2	450	2.49	1.39	13.04**	61.1	9.10**
Sex (S)	1	482	2.67	.22	2.09	3.4	<1
M × D	2	463	2.57	.07	<1	12.6	1.88
M × G	4	238	1.32	.27	2.50*	16.4	2.44*
M × S	2	226	1.25	.03	<1	5.7	<1
D × G	2	308	1.70	.01	<1	.5	<1
D × S	1	52	<1	.09	<1	.6	<1
G × S	2	227	1.26	.01	<1	.9	<1
M × D × G	4	526	2.91*	.17	1.63	8.5	1.27
M × D × S	2	157	<1	.12	1.14	.7	<1
M × G × S	4	212	1.17	.13	1.22	9.1	1.36
D × G × S	2	74	<1	.00	<1	.8	<1
M × D × G × S	4	59	<1	.11	1.01	11.4	1.71
Error (B)	180	181		.11		6.7	

*p < .05.
**p < .001.

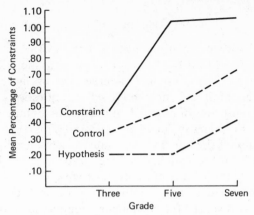

Fig. 1 Model × Grade interaction for the percentage of constraints over two problems.

from the control. For the fifth graders there was a higher percentage of constraints with the constraint-seeking model than the control ($p < .001$) or hypothesis-scanning model ($p < .001$), and more for the control than the hypothesis-scanning model ($p < .01$). The same pattern held for the seventh graders. For the hypothesis-scanning model seventh graders had a higher percentage of constraints than fifth ($p < .01$) or third ($p < .01$) graders, who did not differ. For the constraint-seeking model both seventh and fifth graders had a higher percentage of constraints than third graders ($p < .001$), but did not differ from each other. For the control conditions seventh graders had a higher percentage of constraints than either fifth ($p < .05$) or third ($p < .001$) graders, who did not differ.

Thus, in summary, for the third graders the use of the more efficient strategy of constraint seeking was neither increased by the constraint-seeking model nor decreased by the hypothesis-scanning model relative to the control, while for the fifth and seventh graders there was more use of the strategy with the constraint-seeking model and less with the hypothesis-scanning model relative to the control. Likewise, the seventh graders were better able to resist the influence of the hypothesis-scanning model than the fifth graders. Thus, the influence of the model in both facilitating and hindering the use of a more efficient strategy was most pronounced for the fifth graders.

Average Number of Items Included per Question

This measure considered the number of items included in each question asked. A specific hypothesis included one item, while a constraint could include two or more. The total number of items included over all questions asked was divided by the number of questions to obtain the average number of items included per question. This measure was thus an index of the information value of each question, or, alternatively, of the "quality" of the constraints. As indicated in Table 2, the results of analysis of variance for this measure corresponded exactly to those for the percentage of constraints. Also, the further Duncan comparisons corresponded exactly to those for the percentage of constraints, and hence they are not further reported. This correspondence of the two measures is also indicated by their high correlations in Table 3.

Table 3 Correlations Between Number of Questions, Percentage of Constraints, and Average Items per Question, for Totals over Two Problems, Within Grade Levels, and Within Model Conditions

ITEM	NUMBER OF QUESTIONS AND PERCENTAGE OF CONSTRAINTS	NUMBER OF QUESTIONS AND AVERAGE ITEMS PER QUESTION	PERCENTAGE OF CONSTRAINTS AND AVERAGE ITEMS PER QUESTION
Grade			
Three	.05 (.16)	−.14 (−.07)	.57 (.58)
Five	−.30 (−.29)	−.14 (.10)	.70 (.69)
Seven	−.74 (−.65)	−.48 (.17)	.75 (.67)
Total	−.33 (−.19)	−.28 (−.07)	.71 (.68)
Model			
Hypothesis	−.16 (.11)	−.30 (−.28)	.76 (.76)
Constraint	−.30 (−.12)	−.31 (−.14)	.71 (.68)
Control	−.39 (−.38)	−.16 (.11)	.61 (.60)

Note. Partial correlations with the third variable partialed out are given in parentheses.

Correlations Between Response Measures

The correlations between the three response measures are given in Table 3. Partial correlations with the third variable partialed out are given in parentheses after each correlation.

DISCUSSION

h

The basic finding was the pronounced influence of observing the information-processing strategy employed by the adult model on the subsequent strategy employed by the child. Thus, observation of the constraint-seeking model resulted in a higher percentage of constraint questions than the controls who did not observe the model, and observation of the hypothesis-scanning model resulted in a lower percentage of constraints than the controls. Furthermore, children who observed the more efficient constraint-seeking strategy solved the problems in fewer questions than the controls, while those who observed the less efficient hypothesis-scanning strategy required more questions than the controls. This

i supports the emphasis of Bandura and Walters (1963) upon the importance of the model in learning, and indicates that the model can both facilitate and hinder performance. Again,

j analyses of the significant Model × Grade interaction indicated that the influence of the model was relatively more important for the fifth graders than for the third or seventh graders. This interaction extends the expected result that the use of the constraint-seeking strategy increased directly with school grade (Bruner et al., 1966). Finally, the influence of the model parallels and extends the finding of Bruner et al., that performance was better in "constrained conditions," in which their Ss were asked after each question whether or not they had sufficient information to solve the problem, than in "free conditions," in which nothing was said after each question.

The results for average number of items per question, which may be considered a measure of the information value of each question, or of the "quality" or comprehensiveness of each constraint, corresponded exactly to the results for the percentage of constraints. Thus, the dichotomous measure of

k a constraint versus a specific hypothesis for each question gave the same results as a more elaborate information analysis. In other words, the presence or absence of the ability to categorize objects into logical or functional groups and to use these groupings as a basis of constraint questions was as important as the specific type of constraint questions formulated. Finally, the nonsignificant difference between the pictorial and verbal displays indicates that this dichotomous presence or absence of the ability to use constraints was equally important in the more abstract displays of words and the more concrete displays of drawings.

REFERENCES

Bandura, A. Vicarious processes: A case of no-trial learning. In L. Berkowitz (Ed.), *Advances in experimental social psychology*. Vol. 2. New York: Academic Press, 1965.

Bandura, A., & Walters, R. W. *Social learning and personality development*. New York: Holt, Rinehart & Winston, 1963.

Bruner, J. S., Olver, R. R., & Greenfield, P. M. *Studies in cognitive growth*. New York: Wiley, 1966.

Walters, R. W., & Parke, R. D. Social motivation, dependency, and susceptibility to social influence. In L. Berkowitz (Ed.), *Advances in experimental social psychology*. Vol. 1. New York: Academic Press, 1964.

CASE ANALYSIS

Most college students have participated in the game of "20 questions." The procedure is simple—one person thinks of something, place, or person and identifies it as either animal, vegetable, or mineral. The other players then ask up to 20 questions which can be answered by "yes" or "no." If someone correctly identifies the object within 20 questions, he wins and is normally given the opportunity to think up a new object.

Some psychologists have suggested that man's cognitive processes can be accurately studied by analyzing the questions he asks. In an excellent example of elucidating children's cognitive processes, Laughlin *et al.* employ the method of analyzing the types of questions asked by children who have observed adults ask various types of questions.

This article fits into a long history of experiments which have attempted to identify the specific processes involved in thinking. The Greek philosophers asked "How do we know?" Early nineteenth-century European psychologists tried to isolate the functions of the sensory processes; Helmholtz described his own thought process by means of introspection. Contemporary work on thinking and information processing is conspicuously experimental in nature. In the article by Laughlin, Moss, and Miller you will notice that several independent variables are manipulated and the results of the variables are carefully and unambiguously recorded. From a methodological standpoint, the article represents a multi-level factorial design in which many factors are considered in a single statistical procedure.

REVIEW

The authors of this research paper briefly review the technique previously employed and then identify critical strategies observed in a previous study (**a**). These two problem-solving methods, hypothesis-scanning and constraint-seeking, are defined and examples of each method are given. Laughlin *et al.* assert that not only do the different strategies reflect a change from perceptual to functional thinking but also may be concomitant of age variations (**b**).

A second concept is introduced in (**c**) in which learning among children is thought to be largely imitative rather than the buildup of small reinforced responses. In (**d**) the purpose of this study is clearly and unambiguously stated.

METHOD

In the section on factorial designs (Chapter 2), it was indicated that researchers frequently manipulate two or more variables at the same time. In that chapter the most complex design that was illustrated was a 2 × 4 design. In the Laughlin *et al.* article, five factors are being manipulated at the same time, so the design is considerably more complex than those previously discussed.

However, the logic of the design and the analysis of the data is quite similar to those presented in Chapter 2 and we suggest that the student reread pp. 22–29 on factorial design before analyzing the Method section of the present article.

The design is a $3 \times 2 \times 3 \times 2 \times 2$ design. The first factor was the model factor and consisted of three levels. Prior to the subject actually solving the problems, either (1) an adult model solved a practice problem using a hypothesis-scanning strategy, (2) an adult model solved a practice problem using a constraint-seeking strategy, or (3) the subject solved the practice problem without help of a model. This last treatment was a control treatment (no model). Note that subject actually worked the practice problem in this control treatment. This controls for an "exposure to problems" variable in that all subjects are exposed to a practice problem but only two treatment groups see an adult model actually solve the problem.

The second factor was the stimulus display factor, and this consisted of two levels. Half of the subjects saw the stimulus objects in pictorial form (e.g., a picture of a cow) and the other half of the subjects were given verbal displays of the same objects (e.g., the word *cow*).

The third factor was the grade level of the subjects and this consisted of three levels. One-third of the subjects were from the third grade, one-third of the subjects were from the fifth grade, and one-third of the subjects were from the seventh grade.

The fourth factor was the sex of the subject and (as seems biologically evident) this factor consisted of two levels. One-half of the subjects were male and the other half of the subjects were female.

The fifth factor was the problem factor. Each subject solved two problems. This was the "repeated-measures" aspect of the design. In all of the other factors different subjects are being tested at each level. For this factor all subjects were tested at both "levels." Thus the subjects at one "level" are repeated at a second "level."

Th design necessitated 36 different treatment groups ($3 \times 2 \times 3 \times 2$). No additional treatment groups were needed for the last factor since all subjects were participating at both "levels" of this factor. The experimenters *randomly* assigned six subjects to each of the 36 treatment groups. The experimenters do not state how this random assignment was accomplished; however, we assume it was using one of the techniques discussed in Chapter 5 and is an attempt to equalize subject characteristics in each of the 36 treatments. The design necessitated the use of 216 subjects (6 × 36).

In (e) the authors describe how the stimulus materials were presented to the subject. The actual problems were presented to the subjects on a large board which contained 42 objects arranged in six rows and seven columns. The practice problem (or sample problem) consisted of only 16 objects mounted on a board and arranged in four rows and four columns. The authors also refer to a previous reference (Bruner *et al.*, 1966) which provides a more ample explanation of the stimulus objects used.

The authors next repeat the exact instructions that were given to the subjects so that the reader will know exactly how the task was posed to the subjects. This allows the experiment to be replicated using the same instructions. The authors also state when the problem was scored as correct. In the last sentence of the Method section they note that four experimenters were used, two males and two females, who each ran a proportionate number of subjects in each of the 36 treatments. Using both male and female experimenters is a very important control consideration instituted by the authors since there is some evidence that the sex of the experimenter may affect the performance of children. At least one study showed that children perform better with opposite sex experimenters than with same sex experimenters, e.g., boys perform better with female experimenters than with male experimenters. The authors of the present study controlled for this possible extraneous variable by using both male and female experimenters and by having experimenters of each sex run an equal number of subjects in each of the 36 treatments. Actually the authors could have added the sex of the experimenter as another (the sixth) factor in their design. We can only speculate that they did not because they were not particularly interested in this factor and the design was already quite complex.

Since there were four different experimenters it is also important to control for their characteristics. If one experimenter had run all subjects in one treatment and a different experimenter had run all subjects in a second treatment, we would not be sure if the differences found on the dependent variable were due to the two different treatments or to the two different experimenters. To control for this problem all four experimenters ran a proportionate number of subjects in each of the 36 treatments. Note that each experimenter could not run an *equal* number of subjects in each treatment since there are four experiments and six subjects. Most probably one male experimenter and one female experimenter each ran two subjects in each treatment, and the other male and the other female experimenter each ran one subject in each treatment.

RESULTS

Because of the complexity of this design a great amount of data was generated. The authors present all pertinent data in Tables 1, 2, and 3. It would be redundant to report the same information in the text, so Laughlin *et al.* uses the text for two purposes. The first is to report the results of certain statistical procedures and the second is to emphasize selected results which are reported in the tables.

The repeated measures results were statistically nonsignificant and were eliminated from Table 1. If you look at Table 1, you will notice it is a tabled form of a factorial study which is consistent with the design. The design was a $3 \times 2 \times 3 \times 2$ (eliminating the last repeated-measure factor). The *3* corresponds to the major headings: hypothesis-scanning, constraint-seeking, and control. Within each of the 3 major categories there are 2 subcategories: pictorial and verbal; and 3 sub-subcategories: grades 3, 5, and 7; and finally 2 sub-sub-subcategories: male and female. Study this table for a more complete understanding of the categories in a factorial design.

Table 2 is a summary of the overall analysis of variance of this study. If you have not studied statistics, this table may be a bit bewildering. However, you should be able to note the major features of the analysis from the previous discussion of analysis of variance presented on p. 25. First note that there are three dependent variables: (1) number of questions asked before the problem was solved, (2) the percentage of constraints used, and (3) items per question. The authors analyze each dependent variable separately, and they devote a separate section to each dependent variable which also includes an operational definition of each of the three. In Table 2 the results of the analysis of variance are summarized. As you read down the first column (Source) you first note the results of the main effect of model (M): "Did the model treatments make a difference in performance?" The next is the main effect of display (D): "Was there a difference in performance as a function of the two types of displays?" The next row summarizes the analysis of main effect of grade: "Was there a difference in performance as a function of the grade level of the subjects?" The next row summarizes the analysis of the main effect of sex: "Was the performance of males different from that of females?"

The rest of the table contains the analysis of the interaction effects. For example, the first interaction is a model-by-display interaction and this asks the question of whether or not the model treatments had a different effect on performance as a function of the type of stimulus display. Examine the table with particular attention to the "statistically significant" effects, i.e., those marked with a single or double asterisk. It is these effects that are singled out for emphasis in the text. For example, the (M) factor was found to be statistically significant, i.e., there are differences in performance as a function of the model treatment. However, the analysis of variance does not tell you exactly which of the three treatments differs from the others and the authors use another statistical test (f) to see exactly where the differences lie.

One significant interaction was singled out, reanalyzed in (g), interpreted in the next paragraph, and presented in Fig. 1. The authors apparently feel that this interaction is quite important and have taken care to insure that the reader understands it.

The last paragraph within this section notes that the correlations between the three response measures are given in Table 3. There are three dependent variables in this study, or perhaps better expressed, there are three measures of the subject's performance. The question should be raised as to what is the relationship between the three measures. Are they highly correlated with one another and can be actually treated as a single measure or are they really measuring different aspects of performance? Table 3 presents the relevant data. It appears that percentage of constraints and average items per question are essentially measuring the same dimension; however, the correlation between these two response measures is not quite high enough to have allowed the authors to drop one of the two measures from their analysis.

DISCUSSION

If you found the results of this study obscured by the myriad of statistics, you can be relieved for there can be no doubt of the basic finding of this study after reading (**h**). An adult model acts as a powerful determinant in a child's selection of problem-solving strategies. In (**i**) the writers refer to the hypothesis proposed by Bandura and Walters.

The significant interaction between Model and Grade is interpreted (**j**) as indicating that the model had greater impact on fifth-grade subjects than on third- or seventh-grade subjects.

In the final paragraph (**k**) Laughlin speculates as to the relative importance of the ability to categorize objects versus specific questions asked by subjects in problem solving. Like all good research, this study raises questions as well as answering them.

QUESTIONS

1.   What implications do you see in the Model X Grade interaction?

2.   Draw a graph of the number of questions for the three models with grades (3, 5, and 7) along the horizontal axes. (Combine male and female scores and pictorial and verbal scores.)

3.   Which of the four major factors yielded significant data? Is the nonsignificant data useful? Why? Why not?

4.   Briefly design another study in which a different problem-solving model serves as an independent variable.

5.   The authors found support for the theoretical formulation of children's learning as expressed by Bandura and Walters but did not offer contrary evidence of so-called "reinforcement theories." Propose a study in which a reinforcement theory of information processing is tested.

6.   Does this research have implications for educational practice? How might you apply the ideas in this paper to a college course in experimental psychology? A course in mathematics? In poetry writing?

7.   What value would instruction in constraint-seeking in addition to the model have on information processing?

8.   With frequent repetition of information-processing problems without a model would a constraint strategy develop? What might be the long-term effects of this technique? What implications would the results have for the development of problem-solving skill in children?

14

SHORT-TERM RETENTION

SHORT-TERM RETENTION OF INDIVIDUAL VERBAL ITEMS

Lloyd R. Peterson
and Margaret Jean Peterson
Indiana University

It is apparent that the acquisition of verbal habits depends on the effects of a given occasion being carried over into later repetitions of the situation. Nevertheless, textbooks separate acquisition and retention into distinct categories. The limitation of discussions of retention to long-term characteristics is

a

necessary in large part by the scarcity of data on the course of retention over intervals of the order of magnitude of the time elapsing between successive repetitions in an acquisition study. The presence of a retentive function within the acquisition process was postulated by Hull (1940) in his use of the stimulus trace to explain serial phenomena. Again, Underwood (1949) has suggested that forgetting occurs during the acquisition process. But these theoretical considerations have not led to empirical investigation. Hull (1952) quantified the stimulus trace on data concerned with the CS-UCS interval in eyelid conditioning and it is not obvious that the construct so quantified can be readily transferred to verbal learning. One objection is that a verbal stimulus produces a strong predictable response prior to the experimental session and this is

Reprinted by permission from *Journal of Experimental Psychology*, 1959, *58*, 193–198. Published by the American Psychological Association.

not true of the originally neutral stimulus in eyelid conditioning.

Two studies have shown that the effects of verbal stimulation can decrease over intervals measured in seconds. Pillsbury and Sylvester (1940) found marked decrement with a list of items tested for recall 10 sec. after a single presentation. However, it seems unlikely that this traditional presentation of a list and later testing for recall of the list will be useful in studying intervals near or shorter than the time necessary to present the list. Of more interest is a recent study by Brown (1958) in which among other conditions a single pair of consonants was tested after a 5-sec. interval. Decrement was found at the one recall interval, but no systematic study of the course of retention over a variety of intervals was attempted.

EXPERIMENT I

b The present investigation tests recall for individual items after several short intervals. An item is presented and tested without related items intervening. The initial study examines **c** the course of retention after one brief presentation of the item.

METHOD

Subjects.   The Ss were 24 students from introductory psychology courses at Indiana University. Participation in experiments was a course requirement.

Materials.   The verbal items tested for recall were 48 consonant **d** syllables with Witmer association value no greater than 33 percent (Hilgard, 1951). Other materials were 48 three-digit numbers obtained from a table of random numbers. One of these was given to S after each presentation under instructions to count backward from the number. It was considered that continuous verbal activity during the time between presentation and signal for recall was desirable in **e** order to minimize rehearsal behavior. The materials were selected to be categorically dissimilar and hence involve a minimum of interference.

Procedure.   The S was seated at a table with E seated facing in the same direction on S's right. A black plywood screen shielded E from S. On the table in front of S were two small lights mounted on a black box. The general procedure was for E to spell a consonant syllable and immediately speak a three-digit number. The *S* then counted backward by three or four from this number. On flashing of a signal light *S* attempted to recall the consonant syllable. The *E* spoke in rhythm with a metronome clicking twice per second and *S* was instructed to do likewise. The timing of these events is diagrammed in Fig. 1. As *E* spoke the third digit, he pressed a button activating a Hunter interval timer. At the end of a preset interval the timer activated a red light and an electric clock. The light was the signal for recall. The clock ran until *E* heard *S* speak three letters, when *E* stopped the clock by depressing a key. This time between onset of the light and completion of a response will be referred to as latency. It is to be distinguished from the interval from completion of the syllable by *E* to onset of the light, which will be referred to as the recall interval.

The instructions read to *S* were as follows:

> Please sit against the back of your chair so that you are comfortable. You will not be shocked during this experiment. In front of you is a little black box. The top or green light is on now. This green light means that we are ready to begin a trial. I will speak some letters and then a number. You are to repeat the number immediately after I say it and begin counting backwards by 3's (4's) from that number in time with the ticking that you hear. I might say, ABC 309. Then you say, 309, 306, 303, etc., until the bottom or red light comes on. When you see this red light come on, stop counting immediately and say the letters that were given at the beginning of the trial. Remember to keep your eyes on the black box at all times. There will be a short rest period and then the green light will come on again and we will start a new trial.

The *E* summarized what he had already said and then gave *S* two practice trials. During this practice *S* was corrected if he hesitated before starting to count, or if he failed to stop counting on signal, or if he in any other way deviated from the instructions.

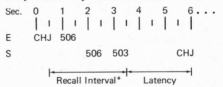

Fig. 1 Sequence of events for a recall interval of 3 sec.

Each S was tested eight times at each of the recall intervals, 3, 6, 9, 12, 15, and 18 sec. A given consonant syllable was used only once with each S. Each syllable occurred equally often over the group at each recall interval. A specific recall interval was represented once in each successive block of six presentations. The S counted backward by three on half of the trials and by four on the remaining trials. No two successive items contained letters in common. The time between signal for recall and the start of the next presentation was 15 sec.

f

Results and Discussion

Responses occurring any time during the 15-sec. interval following signal for recall were recorded. In Fig. 2 are plotted the proportions of correct recalls as cumulative functions of latency for each of the recall intervals. Sign tests were used to evaluate differences among the curves (Walker & Lev, 1953). At each latency differences among the 3-, 6-, 9-, and 18-sec. recall interval curves are significant at the .05 level. For latencies of 6 sec. and longer these differences are all significant at the .01 level. Note that the number correct with latency less than 2 sec. does not constitute a majority of the total correct. These responses would not seem appropriately described as identification of the gradually weakening trace of a stimulus. There is a suggestion of an oscillatory characteristic in the events determining them.

The feasibility of an interpretation by a statistical model was explored by fitting to the data the exponential curve of Fig. 3. The empirical points plotted here are proportions of correct responses with latencies shorter than 2.83 sec. Partition of the correct responses on the basis of latency is required by considerations developed in detail by Estes (1950). A given probability of response applies to an interval of time equal in length to the average time required for the response under consideration to occur. The mean latency of correct responses in the present experiment was 2.83 sec. Differences among the proportions of correct responses with latencies shorter than 2.83 sec. were evaluated by sign tests. The difference between the 3- and 18-sec. conditions was found to be significant at the .01 level. All differences among the 3-, 6-, 9-, 12-, and 18-sec. conditions were significant at the .05 level.

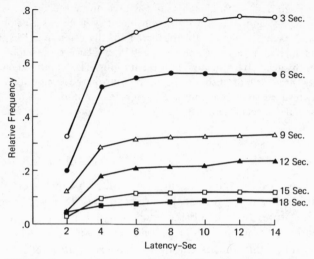

Fig. 2   Correct recalls as cumulative functions of latency.

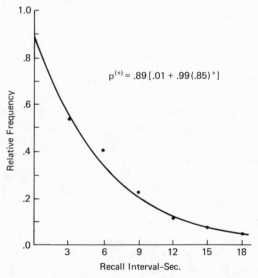

Fig. 3   Correct recalls with latencies below 2.83 sec. as a function of recall interval.

The general equation of which the expression for the curve of Fig. 3 is a specific instance is derived from the stimulus fluctuation model developed by Estes (1955). In applying the model to the present experiment it is assumed that the verbal stimulus produces a response in S which is conditioned to a set of elements contiguous with the response. The elements thus reconditioned are a sample of a larger population of elements into which the conditioned elements disperse as time passes. The proportion of conditioned elements in the sample determining S's behavior thus decreases and with it the probability of the response. Since the fitted curve appears to do justice to the data, the observed decrement could arise from stimulus fluctuation.

The independence of successive presentations might be questioned in the light of findings that performance deteriorates as a function of previous learning (Underwood, 1957). The presence of proactive interference was tested by noting **g** the correct responses within each successive block of 12 presentations. The short recall intervals were analyzed separately from the long recall intervals in view of the possibility that facilitation might occur with the one and interference with the other. The proportions of correct responses for the combined 3- and 6-sec. recall intervals were in order of occurrence .57, .66, .70, and .74. A sign test showed the difference between the first and last blocks to be significant at the .02 level. The proportions correct for the 15- and 18-sec. recall intervals were .08, .15, .09, and .12. The gain from first to last blocks is **h** not significant in this case. There is no evidence for proactive interference. There is an indication of improvement with practice.

EXPERIMENT II

The findings in Exp. I are compatible with the proposition that the after-effects of a single, brief, verbal stimulation can be interpreted as those of a trial of learning. It would be predicted from such an interpretation that probability of recall at **i** a given recall interval should increase as a function of repetitions of the stimulation. Forgetting should proceed at differential rates for items with differing numbers of repetitions.

Although this seems to be a reasonable prediction, there are those who would predict otherwise. Brown (1958), for instance, questions whether repetitions, as such, strengthen the "memory trace." He suggests that the effect of repetitions of **j** a stimulus, or rehearsal, may be merely to postpone the onset of decay of the trace. If time is measured from the moment that the last stimulation ceased, then the forgetting curves should **k** coincide in all cases, no matter how many occurrences of the stimulation have preceded the final occurrence. The second experiment was designed to obtain empirical evidence relevant to this problem.

METHOD

The Ss were 48 students from the source previously described. Half of the Ss were instructed to repeat the stimulus aloud in time with the metronome until stopped by E giving them a number from **l** which S counted backward. The remaining Ss were not given instructions concerning use of the interval between E's presentation of the stimulus and his speaking the number from which to count backward. Both the "vocal" group and the "silent" group had equated intervals of time during which rehearsal inevitably occurred in the one case and could occur in the other case. Differences in frequency of recalls between the groups would indicate a failure of the uninstructed Ss to rehearse. The zero point marking the beginning of the recall interval for the silent group was set at the point at which E spoke the number from which S counted backward. This was also true for the vocal group.

The length of the rehearsal period was varied for Ss of both groups over three conditions. On a third of the presentations S was not given time for any repetitions. This condition was thus comparable to Exp. I, save that the only recall intervals used were 3, 9, and 18 sec. On another third of the presentations 1 sec. elapsed during which S could repeat the stimulus. On another third of the presentations 3 sec. elapsed, or sufficient time for three repetitions. Consonant syllables were varied as to the rehearsal interval in which they were used, so that each syllable occurred equally often in each condition over the group. However, a given syllable was never presented more than once to any S. The Ss were assigned in **m** order of appearance to a randomized list of conditions. Six practice presentations were given during which corrections were made of departures from instructions. Other details follow the procedures of Exp. I.

Results and Discussion

Table 1 shows the proportion of items recalled correctly. In the vocal group recall improved with repetition at each of the recall intervals tested. Conditions in the silent group were not consistently ordered. For purposes of statistical analysis the recall intervals were combined with each group. A sign test between numbers correct in the 0- and 3-repetition conditions of the vocal group showed the difference to be significant at the .01 level. The difference between the corresponding conditions of the silent group was not significant at the .05 level. Only under conditions where repetition of the stimulus was controlled by instructions did retention improve.

Table 1 Proportions of Items Correctly Recalled in Exp. II

GROUP	REPETITION TIME (SEC.)	RECALL INTERVAL (SEC.)		
		3	9	18
	3	.80	.48	.34
Vocal	1	.68	.34	.21
	0	.60	.25	.14
	3	.70	.39	.30
Silent	1	.74	.35	.22
	0	.72	.38	.15

The obtained differences among the zero conditions of Exp. II and the 3-, 9-, and 18-sec. recall intervals of Exp. I require some comment, since procedures were essentially the same. Since these are between-S comparisons, some differences would be predicted because of sampling variability. But another factor is probably involved. There were 48 presentations in Exp. I and only 36 in Exp. II. Since recall was found to improve over successive blocks of trials, a superiority in recall for Ss of Exp. I is reasonable. In the case of differences between the vocal and silent groups of Exp. II a statistical test is permissable, for Ss were assigned randomly to the two groups. Wilcoxon's (1949) test for unpaired replicates, as well as a *t* test, was used. Neither showed significance at the .05 level.

The 1- and 3-repetition conditions of the vocal group afforded an opportunity to obtain a measure of what recall would be at the zero interval in time. It was noted whether a syllable had been correctly repeated by S. Proportions correctly repeated were .90 for the 1-repetition condition and .88 for the 3-repetition condition. The chief source of error lay in the confusion of the letters "m" and "n." This source of error is not confounded with the repetition variable, for it is S who repeats and thus perpetuates his error. Further, individual items were balanced over the three conditions. There is no suggestion of any difference in responding among the repetition conditions at the beginning of the recall interval. These differences developed during the time that S was engaged in counting backward. A differential rate of forgetting seems indisputable.

The factors underlying the improvement in retention with repetition were investigated by means of an analysis of the status of elements within the individual items. The individual consonant syllable, like the nonsense syllable, may be regarded as presenting S with a serial learning task. Through repetitions unrelated components may develop serial dependencies until in the manner of familiar words they have become single units. The improved retention might then be attributed to increases in these serial dependencies. The analysis proceeded by ascertaining the dependent probabilities that letters would be correct given the event that the previous letter was correct. These dependent probabilities are listed in Table 2. It is clear that with increasing repetitions the serial dependencies increase. Again combining recall intervals, a sign test between the zero condition and the three repetition condition is significant at the .01 level.

Learning is seen to take place within the items. But this finding does not eliminate the possibility that another kind of learning is proceeding concurrently. If only the correct occurrences of the first letters of syllables are considered, changes in retention apart from the serial dependencies can be assessed.

Table 2 Dependent Probabilities of a Letter Being Correctly Recalled in the Vocal Group When the Preceding Letter Was Correct

REPETITION TIME (SEC.)	RECALL INTERVAL (SEC.)		
	3	9	18
3	.96	.85	.72
1	.90	.72	.57
0	.86	.64	.56

The proportions of first letters recalled correctly for the 0-, 1-, and 3-repetition conditions were .60, .65, and .72, respectively. A sign test between the 0- and 3-repetition conditions was significant at the .05 level. It may tentatively be concluded that learning of a second kind took place.

The course of short-term verbal retention is seen to be related to learning processes. It would not appear to be strictly accurate to refer to retention after a brief presentation as a stimulus trace. Rather, it would seem appropriate to refer to it as the result of a trial of learning. However, in spite of possible objections to Hull's terminology the present investigation supports his general position that a short-term retentive factor is important for the analysis of verbal learning. The details of the role of retention in the acquisition process remain to be worked out.

SUMMARY

The investigation differed from traditional verbal retention studies in concerning itself with individual items instead of lists. Forgetting over intervals measured in seconds was found. The course of retention after a single presentation was related to a statistical model. Forgetting was found to progress at differential rates dependent on the amount of controlled rehearsal of the stimulus. A portion of the improvement in recall with repetitions was assigned to serial learning within the item, but a second kind of learning was also found. It was concluded that short-term retention is an important, though neglected, aspect of the acquisition process.

REFERENCES

Brown, J. Some tests of the decay theory of immediate memory. *Quart. J. exp. Psychol.*, 1958, *10*, 12–21.

Estes, W. K. Toward a statistical theory of learning. *Psychol. Rev.*, 1950, *57*, 94–107.

Estes, W. K. Statistical theory of spontaneous recovery and regression. *Psychol. Rev.*, 1955, *62*, 145–154.

Hilgard, E. R. Methods and procedures in the study of learning. In S. S. Stevens (Ed.), *Handbook of experimental psychology*. New York: Wiley, 1951.

Hull, C. L., Hovland, C. I., Ross, R. T., Hall, M., Perkins, D. T., & Fitch, F. B. *Mathematico-deductive theory of rote learning: A study in scientific methodology*. New Haven: Yale Univer. Press, 1940.

Hull, C. L. *A behavior system*. New Haven: Yale Univer. Press, 1952.

Pillsbury, W. B., & Sylvester, A. Retroactive and proactive inhibition in immediate memory. *J. exp. Psychol.*, 1940, *27*, 532–545.

Underwood, B. J. *Experimental psychology*. New York: Appleton-Century-Crofts, 1949.

Underwood, B. J. Interference and forgetting. *Psychol. Rev.*, 1957, *64*, 49–60.

Walker, H., & Lev, J. *Statistical inference*. New York: Holt, 1953.

Wilcoxon, F. *Some rapid approximate statistical procedures*. New York: Amer. Cyanamid Co., 1949.

CASE ANALYSIS

What is the name of the city you were born in? Easy, you may say. What is the name of the city your father was born in? That is a bit harder. What city was your grandfather born in? It would be surprising if you knew. All of these examples illustrate memory and its counterpart—forgetting. A dimension common to all of these questions and which may account for their increasing difficulty, is the frequency with which you have rehearsed the answers. All citizens are frequently asked their place of birth and occasionally asked their parents' place of birth, but rarely asked their grandparents' place of birth.

If repetition is the basis of memory, then you may reason, if a subject had no opportunity to rehearse material he would have no permanent memory. Suppose you looked up the telephone number of an acquaintance. The number may be retained only long enough for the call to be completed—and in some cases not even that long. A few minutes later you cannot recall the number at all.

It appears from many different types of evidence that there are two distinct types of memory. One develops after many repetitions and persists for some time and another is transitory in nature and develops after only a few repetitions. The distinction between short-term memory and long-term memory is widely accepted by psychologists.

The article by Peterson and Peterson stimulated considerable activity in the field of short-term memory partly because it involves a new methodology. The previous technique of measuring short-term memory of verbal material was to present the subject with an entire list of words or nonsense syllables. Retention of the entire list was then measured. The Petersons' design sharply reduced the possibility of a facilitating interaction among the verbal stimuli. For example, a serial list containing the following words: *boy, dog, leg, face, auto* could easily be encoded into "The *boy*'s *dog* broke his *leg* as he *faced* the *auto*." However, if each item was individually presented (e.g., *boy*) and then recalled, no facilitating or impeding stimuli could influence the results.

Another important feature of the Peterson and Peterson design is the means they used to prevent rehearsal. In the above example nearly everyone would be able to hold in his immediate memory a word for an extended time if he had the opportunity to rehearse the word. The present experimenters prevented their subjects from rehearsing by requiring them to count backwards by 3's after the verbal stimulus was presented. The results and technique used in the Petersons' experiment have had a provocative effect on recent concepts in memory and retention.

Innovative research in psychology is frequently met with both applause *and* criticism. Peterson and Peterson were confronted with an attack on their experiment which suggested that their experimental design did not control for interference which may have occurred when the subject was counting backwards by 3's. The critics (Keppel and Underwood, 1962) argued that the rapid "forgetting" was not only a function of time without rehearsal but was a function of previous learning or proactive inhibition. Proactive inhibition is a condition deleterious to present learning caused by previous associations. The controversy is far from over and as you read the experiment you may appreciate the complexities of designing an experiment devoid of methodological flaws.

EXPERIMENT I:

Peterson and Peterson note in the first paragraph that the psychological literature on retention is limited to long-term retention (**a**). Some theories have been presented regarding short-term memory but much more needs to be done.

This article contains two experiments in which each one contributes to the main problem discussed in the review. In (**b**) an abbreviated statement of the procedure is made and in (**c**) the authors identify the specific procedure used in Experiment I.

Method

Several design issues in this experiment are worth considering. The subjects are identified by their number, occupation, class they were taking, and by what means the experimenter was able to use their services. No mention is made of sex, class, age, race, or IQ. Are these variables important?

There is a clear identification of the dependent variable (items recalled) and independent variable (recall interval). Subject performance as related to these variables is illustrated in Fig. 3. Despite these well-delineated variables, this experiment represents one of the most difficult control problems in psychology: What is the influence of experimental experience on results? Peterson and Peterson are cautious to note that the experience of counting backward by 3's may have interfering effects (or facilitating effects) on the dependent variable. The whole story of those pesky subtracted numbers has not yet been told and their influence is still being investigated.

The selection of the materials is a critical part of verbal learning studies. The authors selected the verbal elements composed of three consonants and obviously a nonword (**d**). The consonants had previously been scaled for associativeness, or a measure of the number of associations the verbal element elicits. All CCCs (consonant–consonant–consonant) had a low associative value while three-digit numbers were selected from a table of random numbers. An example of a CCC and a digit used in this study is CHJ and 506. An important rational for the study is mentioned in (**e**) and is based on the notion that subjects cannot rehearse while performing another function. The procedure section explicitly tells what was done. In (**f**) the authors mention a control for possible contamination of the lists. Read it with care and notice the exactness the experimenters use to attempt to measure only the effect of the independent variable.

Results and Discussion

The authors present the results and discussion in the same section. This is an acceptable procedure and is common when multiple experiments are presented in a single article.

Peterson and Peterson effectively present their results in two graphs. In Fig. 2 the correct responses are cumulated per latency of responding after the response signal was given. Of particular interest is the succinct portrayal of the main effects of short-term memory illustrated in Fig. 3, and they relate these results to a model developed by Estes. In studying experimental articles in psychology you may have to review the literature for complete understanding of the authors' rationale. In the original Estes article, response probability was perceived in terms of a mathematical expression. The rationale and derivation of the model are too complex to be reviewed here, but you may wish to pursue this problem by reading the Estes article.

The Petersons found the mean latency of correct responses (2.83 sec.) and graphically presented those responses below that value in Fig. 3. In general, this figure suggests that the recall of a response is a function of the latency between the presentation of the stimulus and its recall. The curve also illustrates that the greatest deleterious effect of response recall was observed in the first few seconds after the stimulus is presented.

In (g) the researchers consider the problem of proactive interference. Their concern is that retention of later items may be interfered with (or facilitated by) the learning of previous items. By using a repeated measure design (each subject received several trials with several independent variables), the influence of proaction is possible. Peterson and Peterson analyze the data from first and last trials and report that no evidence for proaction was found (h). This section of Peterson and Peterson's paper has been criticized and subsequent research by Keppel and Underwood (1962), Murdock (1961, 1964), and Postman (1964) has helped clarify the issue of proactive interference and the effectiveness of the interfering activity.

EXPERIMENT II

Occasionally an experimental psychologist may report the results of two or more experiments in a single article. This practice has gained some recent popularity as the complexity of psychology demands thorough treatment of problems. The second experiment in this article is about the influence of rehearsal on retention of a verbal item.

The authors relate Experiment II with the results obtained in Experiment I (i). This paragraph serves as an effective transition between the two experiments. In (j) there is a brief review of a theory of memory and in (k) they state the problem (and infer an hypothesis) to be tested in Experiment II.

Method

Although this method section is similar to Experiment I, some differences are noted. For example, in (l) two groups of subjects are formed; one group was instructed to vocalize the stimulus while the other half was not instructed to vocalize the stimulus. Presumably, one group actively rehearsed while the other group did not. In (m) the experimenters make an observation regarding the assignment of subjects and practice presentations.

Results and Discussion

Examine Table 1. The careful scientist may have an interest in the specific data in this table although the general information could have been presented in a graphic form.

In (**n**) the authors make a concluding statement in reference to the results of Experiment II.

The remainder of the discussion relates the results of the two experiments to each other and to theories of learning. Of particular interest in this section, from a methodological standpoint, was the subjects' confusion between "m" and "n" (**o**). The experimenter considered the possibility that this problem may have affected the dependent variable. They expose the issue and offer a plausible explanation for the irrelevancy of the error (**p**). The experimenters conclude this experiment with an individual analysis of the syllables used as stimuli in this study (**q**).

QUESTIONS

1.   Why were nonword CCC's used in this experiment? Would you anticipate different results with words? Search the current literature for empirical validation of these questions.

2.   What distinction would you make between short-term memory (STM) and long-term memory (LTM). Now, having made that distinction, design a study testing for STM and another study for LTM.

3.   How did the authors prevent rehearsal? Why was this method criticized?

4.   Define forgetting? Based on your reading of this paper is forgetting caused by time and the "decay" of memory traces or by interfering material?

5.   Draw a curve using data from Table 1 and Table 2.

6.   Why did the experimenters use a practice trial in each experiment? What effects may this have on the outcome?

7.   How could the problem of serial effects be eliminated? What problem may be created by elimination of serial effects? Do you see any relationship between the type of material used (CCCs) and encoding concepts?

BIBLIOGRAPHY

American Psychological Association. *Casebook on ethical standards of psychologists.* Washington, D.C.: American Psychological Association, 1967.

American Psychological Association Council of Editors. *Publication manual of the American Psychological Association.* (Rev. Ed.) Washington, D.C.: American Psychological Association, 1967.

Asch, S. *Social psychology.* Englewood Cliffs, N.J.: Prentice-Hall, 1952.

Ayllon, T. Intensive treatment of psychotic behavior by stimulus satiation and food reinforcement. *Behav. Res. Ther.,* 1963, *1,* 53–61.

Ayllon, T. and Azrin, N. H. *The token economy: A motivational system for therapy and rehabilitation.* New York: Appleton-Century-Crofts, 1968.

Bandler, R. J., Madaras, G. R., and Bem, D. J. Self-observation as a source of pain perception. *J. pers. soc. Psychol.,* *9,* 205–209.

Bayoff, A. G. The experimental social behavior of animals: II. The effect of early isolation of white rats on their competition in swimming. *J. comp. Psychol.,* 1940, *29,* 293–306.

Bitterman, M. E. Thorndike and the problem of animal intelligence. *Amer. Psychol.,* 1969, *24,* 444–453.

Conant, J. B. *Science and common sense.* New Haven, Conn.: Yale University Press, 1951.

Crespi, L. Quantitative variation of incentive and performance in the white rat. *Amer. J. Psychol.,* 1942, *55,* 467–517.

Ehrenfreund, D. and Badia, P. Response strength as a function of drive level and pre- and postshift incentive magnitude. *J. exp. Psychol.,* 1962, *63,* 468–471.

Elliott, M. H. The effect of change of reward on the maze performance of rats. *Univ. Calif. Publ. Psychol.,* 1928, *4,* 19–30.

Ferster, C. B. and Perrott, M. C. *Behavior principles.* New York: Appleton-Century-Crofts, 1968.

Festinger, L. *A theory of cognitive dissonance.* New York: Harper & Row, 1957.

Hilgard, E. R. Pain as a puzzle for psychology and physiology. *Amer. Psychol.*, 1969, *24*, 103–113.

Hirsh, I. J. Audition. In J. B. Sidowski (Ed.), *Experimental methods and instrumentation in psychology.* New York: McGraw-Hill, 1966.

Howes, D. H. and Solomon, R. L. A note on McGuinnes' "Emotionality and perceptual defense." *Psychol. Rev.*, 1950, *57*, 229–234.

Howes, D. H. and Solomon, R. L. Visual duration threshold as a function of word-probability. *J. exp. Psychol.*, 1951, *41*, 401–410.

Johnson, H. H. and Scileppi, J. A. Effects of ego-involvement conditions on attitude change to high and low credibility communicators. *J. pers. soc. Psychol.*, 1969, *13*, 31–36.

Kausler, D. H., Lair, C. V., and Matsumoto, R. Interference transfer paradigms and the performance of schizophrenics and controls. *J. abnorm. soc. Psychol.*, 1964, *69*, 584–587.

Keppel, G. and Underwood, B. J. Proactive inhibition in short-term retention of single items. *J. verb. Learn. verb. Behav.*, 1962, *1*, 153–161.

Lambert, W. W. and Solomon, R. L. Extinction of a running response as a function of block point from the goal. *J. comp. physiol. Psychol.*, 1952, *45*, 269–279.

Laughlin, P. R., Moss, I. L., and Miller, S. M. Information-processing in children as a function of adult model, stimulus display, school grade, and sex. *J. educ. Psychol.*, 1969, *60*, 188–193.

Linder, D. E., Cooper, J., and Jones, E. E. Decision freedom as a determinant of the role of incentive magnitude in attitude change. *J. pers. soc. Psychol.*, 1967, *6*, 245–254.

Lorge, I. Influence of regularly interpolated time intervals upon subsequent learning. *Teach. Coll., Columbia Univer. Contr. Educ.* (whole No. 438), 1930.

More, A. J. Delay of feedback and the acquisition and retention of verbal materials in the classroom. *J. educ. Psychol.*, 1969, *60*, 339–342.

Murdock, B. B., Jr. Proactive inhibition in short-term memory. *J. exp. Psychol.*, 1964, *68*, 184–189.

Murdock, B. B., Jr. Short-term retention of single paired-associates. *Psychol. Rep.*, 1961, *8*, 280.

Paul, G. L. *Insight versus desensitization in psychotherapy.* Stanford, Calif.: Stanford Univ. Press, 1966.

Peterson, L. R. and Peterson, M. J. Short-term retention of individual verbal items. *J. exp. Psychol.*, 1959, *58*, 193–198.

Postman, L. Short-term memory and incidental learning. In A. W. Melton (Ed.), *Categories of human learning.* New York: Academic Press, 1964.

Postman, L., Bronson, W. C., and Gropper, G. L. Is there a mechanism of perceptual defense? *J. abnorm. soc. Psychol.*, 1952, *48*, 215–224.

Pryor, K. W., Haag, R., and O'Reilly, J. The creative porpoise: Training for novel behavior. *J. exp. Anal. Behav.*, 1969, *12*, 653–661.

Simon, C. W. and Emmons, W. H. Responses to material presented during various levels of sleep. *J. Exp. Psychol.*, 1956, *51*, 89–97.

Stevens, S. S. The surprising simplicity of sensory metrics. *Amer. Psychol.*, 1962, *17*, 29–39.

Stevens, S. S. and Davis, H. *Hearing, its psychology and physiology.* New York: Wiley, 1938.

Stevenson, H. W. and Odom, R. D. The effectiveness of social reinforcement following two conditions of social deprivation. *J. abnorm. soc. Psychol.*, 1962, *65*, 429–431.

Supa, M., Cotzin, M., and Dallenbach, K. M. "Facial vision": The perception of obstacles by the blind. *Amer. J. Psychol.*, 1944, *57*, 133–183.

Terkel, J. and Rosenblatt, J. S. Maternal behavior induced by maternal blood plasma injected into virgin rats. *J. comp. physiol. Psychol.*, 1968, *65*, 479–482.

Thumin, F. J. Identification of cola beverages. *J. appl. Psychol.*, 1962, *46*, 358–360.

Underwood, B. J. *Psychological research.* New York: Appleton-Century-Crofts, 1957.

Underwood, B. J., Rehula, R., and Keppel, G. Item selection in paired-associate learning. *Amer. J. Psychol.*, 1962, *75*, 353–371.

Walk, R. D. Two types of depth discrimination by the human infant with five inches of visual depth. *Psychon. Sci.*, 1969, *14*, 253, 254.

Walters, R. H. and Parke, R. D. Emotional arousal, isolation, and discrimination learning in children. *J. exper. child Psychol.*, 1964, *1*, 163–173.

INDEX OF NAMES

INDEX OF SUBJECTS

72 73 74   7 6 5 4 3 2